IN HIS IMAGE

How To Disciple Like Jesus

Justin Heckel

Published by ...Freedom Fellowship Church 5101 s Pennsylvania Ave Oklahoma City OK 73119

Paperback ISBN: 978-1-7368581-8-9
eBook ISBN: 978-1-7368581-9-6

Printed in the United States of America

Book design by Elly Heckel
Cover design by Elly Heckel

Table Of Contents

Justin Heckel

Introduction

I doubt that if any of us were walking with Jesus during His earthly ministry we would say, "You know, I grew for a bit, but then I got stagnant. It was great at the beginning, but then I kind of lost focus." Yet, this happens all the time in the Church. You see people grow for a couple of years and then plateau. Maybe, our focus has just been a bit off.

I started working at the Union Gospel Mission at the beginning of 2021. Part of my job there has been to develop discipleship programs. I had already learned in my life and ministry that there is a vast difference between the way things are typically done in the church and the way they are done in other places in life. When my wife and I stepped out of ministry and into the marketplace, we couldn't do healing and the prophetic in the same way we did it in services. We had to learn how to bring that to people in relatively normal conversation.

I began working on the first round of discipleship. I knew I wanted to build deep intimacy with God and a heart of service into our disciples, but, again, there is a big difference between someone who has a large hunger for God and someone who reluctantly says, "I guess I'll join your program." Within six months, I realized we weren't getting the fruit we wanted. Too much reading, too much head knowledge.

I went back to the drawing board. God asked me, "Do you want them to know a lot or to be transformed?" I am slow on the uptake sometimes, but not that slow. I knew what He was getting at. I had already been diving into some of the works of Dallas Willard and Jim Wilder. I started looking at why discipleship seems to be hit or miss, even in the Church. Why do some people seem to go to church forever but not display being mature followers of Christ?

Above that, I wanted it to be real! I wanted them to learn how to go to God and not just me for the rest of their lives. I wanted them to be so caught up in God that they would save and disciple others. What we are seeing is amazing!

Guys would reluctantly join our program because they knew it would buy them a little more time at the mission. But within a week they would be completely hooked. Guys who had been in and out of prison their whole lives, drug addicts, alcoholics, etc. would give their lives to Jesus, ask non-stop questions, and within a couple of months be going on outreach and leading classes and prayer groups.

It worked so well that we eventually did a run-through online and watched some of the most amazing conversations and spiritual healing take place. It gives a firm foundation on which everything else can be built. I believe the reason why is because what is given here is spiritual science. It's the way God has created everything to work. It will heal you, and give you joy and wisdom. But then the question is, what are you going to do with it?

For example, Jesus said that whoever wants to be the greatest in the Kingdom must be the servant of all. This is the way God created life to work, and how it did until sin entered. Much of the world gains power and authority through control and manipulation. But the way you gain it is the way you have to maintain it. To constantly live that way is exhausting.

The way God made things to work is that as you serve, people hand power and authority over to you. Many neighborhoods in America have an example of this. There is some guy who mows the lawns and shovels the sidewalks of the widow or the person who has just come home from the

3

hospital. If everything went downhill in America, those neighbors would head to that guy's place and ask him what to do. He has authority, not because he said so, but because he served. As you serve people, they want your input on more of their lives because they can trust you.

Because these truths work no matter what, it is important to keep the name of Jesus at the center so that we don't pervert them and lead people to anything else. There are a few premises to all of this. First, of course, you need to know Jesus. Second, you need the baptism of the Holy Spirit. Jesus stressed to His disciples the importance of not carrying on without the Holy Spirit. This pertains to us too, and one reason is simply because He is a better minister and teacher than anybody on this planet. And last, I would say that you must be connected to a group of believers that you can live in fellowship with and be discipled by.

The thought process behind a lot of this stemmed from the book *The Other Half of Church* by Jim Wilder and Michel Hendricks. In short, they explain that we get stuck because we want to give a lot of information, which is analytical. And rightly so because the message of the Kingdom is the seed in the parable of the sower. But the soil determines what happens to that seed. If the message is the seed, then the soil is relationship, abstract thinking, and decision-making.

Therefore, we want to get focused on the relationship. We start with how God wants to restore everything. Then that He wants a deeper relationship with us and how to grow in that.

I don't believe any program is the be-all-end-all. I believe they are a tool. One of the things you'll see early on is stressing that there is no real growth in simply getting head knowledge and that you need to do it in a true discipleship relationship with somebody who can hold you accountable. I want to point out as well that this was originally made for people transitioning out of homelessness and many who have never been a believer. If you are leading a church group through this, there may be pieces that you need to modify or even pass over completely. However, I would say that all of it is beneficial to know.

When we run our programs at the mission, what is written here is a combination of our Core Discipleship and Cultivating the Presence classes. We also have what we call "Purple Book" class. The Purple Book by Rice Broocks and Steve Murrell is a fantastic resource. We use it as our Bible class. Cultivating the Presence is about staying constantly focused on the presence of God and being able to hear Him in every moment for ourselves and others. And then Core Discipleship is about growing as an emotionally and spiritually mature follower of Christ.

I hope as you read this, it brings healing, restoration, understanding, and solidity to your life, relationships, and your walk with God. Jesus is truly the one in whom every mystery and treasure is found. There is nothing better we can do than to stay focused on Him and make disciples of all nations.

CHAPTER 1

What is the purpose of discipleship?

The Kingdom of Heaven Has Drawn Near

"Why do we need to do discipleship? What is the point at all? I go to church! I've read my Bible!" We hear these kinds of things all the time. Yet from the attitudes and behaviors many carry, you would never be able to tell they are followers of Christ. So why do we need discipleship?

We can all probably agree that things in life don't always go as planned, right? Yet, we can watch other people who don't seem to have the issues that we have. And we can find people that not only don't have those issues, but they seem to have those answers conquered. It probably isn't true for every part of their life, but at least for certain pieces.

What is the quickest way for me to conquer them myself? If I wanted to conquer alcoholism, the quickest way for me to get past it would be to get around a bunch of guys who have conquered it themselves. Did you ever notice that guys who are fit tend to hang around other fit guys? They talk about working out nonstop and their diet, etc. If I wanted to get rich, I should probably go hang out with Warren Buffet and do whatever he tells me to do.

The quickest way to win is to find someone with the results we want and to do whatever they say. I may not agree with everything, but how foolish is it to say, "I want what you have, but I don't want to do what you do"? I want to see if I can get the same results.

We said that nobody has all of life figured out, but there is One who does. If you've ever been to Sunday School, you know the answer is Jesus.
1. He is the Way, the Truth, and the Life. (John 14:6)
2. Jesus was the first to model being discipled. **So Jesus said to them, "Truly, truly, I say to you, the Son can do nothing of his own accord, but only what he sees the Father doing. For whatever the Father does, that the Son does likewise. (John 5:19) (ESV)**
3. And when we are in Christ, we also have His Holy Spirit.
   A. **If the Spirit of him who raised Jesus from the dead dwells in you, he who raised Christ Jesus from the dead will also give life to your mortal bodies through his Spirit who dwells in you. (Romans 8:11) (ESV)**
   B. **But the Helper, the Holy Spirit, whom the Father will send in my name, he will teach you all things and bring to your remembrance all that I have said to you. (John 14:26) (ESV)**
   C. **And Jesus' apostles told people, "Follow me as I follow Christ." (1 Corinthians 11:1)**
4. And what did Jesus do? He led us back to the Father. And if we can get to know the Father, we can know our true identity. We can see through our issues. We can know better how things work. Our Father has all the answers. It's one big game of following the leader.

Why are there issues in life? Why do things seem so hard at times?
1. All of our issues in life have been due to things that God never intended to be in the world, but we have come to see them as "normal." If we never see the truth, we will always have confusion. But once we know, we can be intentional.

2. In the creation story, you see that everything God created, He called good.
3. But we also notice right after the creation story that Satan was already in the Garden.
4. We were given authority; the enemy didn't have any. Therefore, he needed to get it from us.

But God's Original Plan Was Different
1. The way God originally planned the world was for us to be agents of wholeness. We would bring order out of chaos. We would be like God to the world.
2. **So God created mankind in his own image, in the image of God he created them; male and female he created them. God blessed them and said to them, "Be fruitful and increase in number; fill the earth and subdue it. Rule over the fish in the sea and the birds in the sky and over every living creature that moves on the ground." (Genesis 1:27, 28) (NIV)**
3. Why was there a need for humans, beings who would bring order? Well, we don't know everything. But we do know that there had been a war that happened in heaven (Revelation 12) and that Satan and his angels had been kicked out of heaven, and were already in the earth.

Now, I want to give some reality to what all of this may have looked like in the Garden of Eden. I have heard many times people ask certain questions like, "Where was Adam when Eve was eating the fruit? Why didn't he step in?" Well, I think if we look at what some of the realities probably are, we can answer a lot of these kinds of questions, and it helps us understand our situation as humans a little better. I'm not saying this is exactly how it was, but it's plausible and helps our understanding.

The word for Satan in the Garden used by the Hebrews is "Nahash" and it can mean three different things that are all applicable, it can mean "serpent", "shining one", or "deceiver". Imagine this fantastic-looking creature, has come into where Adam and Eve are hanging out. Like most guys, Adam is probably making some comparisons and feeling a little outdone by this guy. If Satan is a good deceiver, he isn't just going to come out and say, "Why don't you do that thing God told you not to do?" He has probably been walking around giving off knowledge he has about how the world was made and how different things interact. Now Adam is feeling like, "This guy is super smart too and keeps talking to my girl, so I'm just gonna sit over on the side and keep quiet instead of talking and being outclassed." Seems like what we tend to act like as guys, right?

If Adam would have only realized, he didn't need to engage in a battle of wits. He simply needed to use his authority. He had it. Satan didn't. If he would have simply told him to leave, there wouldn't have been an issue.

And what about Eve? I imagine if she was the helpmate she was created to be, she was thinking, "This guy sounds smart, and this could be good for our home. I know it isn't exactly what we were told, but I want to look at the positive instead of the negative."

Again, if she had stuck to the area, she was given authority instead of being swayed by knowledge, we would be living a different type of life right now. But these are attitudes and habits that are still common to us in so many ways.

The reason I bring up that God never turned away was because we often attribute qualities to God that I couldn't do and still be considered a good dad. An example of this is that I have three boys. Let's say that I take them to a carnival (a chaotic place where danger already is, right?). What would I do if my oldest decides to punch one of my other sons for some reason? If I said, "I can't stand being around you now, I'm leaving you all here," and left, I would have my kids taken away from me for being a horrible father.

But if I discipline my son, I know that he would immediately be upset. Before I even get to it, I know that as soon as he heard my voice say his name, fear would creep in. That voice that had been bringing joy to him all day would suddenly turn into a presence of darkness. As soon as the discipline began, he would think, "Dad doesn't want anything to do with me." I know he would probably want to run away and hide out of shame (just like Adam). I would need to hold his hand to make sure he stayed with me. But then he would turn his back and create a separation in his mind. This is much like Paul says in **Colossians 1:21, "Once you were alienated from God and were enemies in your minds because of your evil behavior." (NIV)**

Because I have other children to think about and I don't want to waste our day at the carnival, I start leading my family over to the next attraction. The whole way my oldest would be trying to dig his heels in and pout. All I am trying to do as a good dad is get the family to the next thing and help the family have a good time, but his mind is stuck back where the incident occurred, and he believes that I am still stuck back there as well.

In fact, what happened right after that? Well, God showed up for the daily walk together. Who are the ones who hid? We were. God still shows up; we are the ones who run away. And we will get into some of the other implications in a bit.

For now, let's ask and answer some questions as to why we are here and why discipleship is important.

1. **Why are we here and why does the world exist?**
   Well, first, the Lord is relational. He doesn't do anything arbitrarily, like create a world for no reason. He already thought of us before He thought about making the world. **Ephesians 1:4 says, "Even as he chose us in him before the foundation of the world, that we should be holy and blameless before him."**

   He thought about manifesting His glory in a physical way, knew how He would wrap it in skin, give it your name, place you at a location in the earth at a specific period in time around specific people so that you could be taken care of AND display His glory in a mighty way. And no matter what has happened, He has never shrunk His expectations of

---

that.

2. **Why would a Good Father put His children in a world where His enemy was?**
A. There is no way that I could put my kids in the same room as an enemy that wanted to end my family line and still be considered a good dad...UNLESS I believed that my kids were more of a threat to the enemy than the enemy was to my kids.

B. That's right, God put us here to be agents of wholeness who bring order to chaos.

C. And we were the ones given authority. And Satan and his fallen angels were a defeated Kingdom that had been cast out.

3. **How did the enemy take away our authority?"**
A. He lied to us.

B. This has wreaked havoc in our lives and caused us to believe all kinds of lies.
   1. **Jesus said, "I have said these things to you, that in me you may have peace. In the world you will have tribulation. But take heart; I have overcome the world." (John 16:33) (ESV)**
   2. Hardship happens because sin entered the world. But the Enemy lies and tells you he did that bad thing in order to make you feel like a victim. He tells you God has turned away from you to make you feel alone. He tells you it happened because you screwed up so that you feel ashamed.
   3. But Jesus has told us to stop listening to the lies. Yes, there are things that have happened, but the enemy was defeated at the cross. And you are not a victim. You are not alone. And He came to take away your shame. He has overcome the pain, fear,

hopelessness, etc. that life's issues have put on you.

So, If we are to be ultimately discipled by Jesus and go back to the Father, this is what Jesus preached.

1. "Repent, for the kingdom of heaven is at hand." (Matthew 3:2) (ESV)
2. Stop believing the lies that God is distant. Heaven has drawn near and is within arms reach.
3. Our Father is a good Father. He doesn't take joy in seeing any of His children fall or be hurt. He doesn't want to zap you with a lightning bolt!
4. **His divine power has given us everything we need for a godly life through our knowledge of him who called us by his own glory and goodness. (2 Peter 1:3) (NIV)**
5. **The thief comes only to steal and kill and destroy. I came that they may have life and have it abundantly. (John 10:10)**

The Best Way to Know Christ

Jesus is the way to know the Father, and people can help us see who Jesus is. But if everybody has fallen short, we need someone who can be consistent in revealing Jesus to us. That job lies directly on one being, the Holy Spirit. **According to John 14:26-27, part of the Holy Spirit's job is to teach us everything and remind us of everything Jesus has said.**

Matthew 7:24-27 says, "Therefore everyone who hears these words of mine and puts them into practice is like a wise man who built his house on the rock. The rain came down, the streams rose, and the winds blew and beat against that house; yet it did not fall, because it had its foundation on the rock." (NIV) There are teachings floating around in the church world that talk about not needing to do this or that because Jesus was your perfect substitute. Well, He was, but He also tells you that to not live according to His words makes you a foolish builder whose house will crash. Notice that both houses experience the same rain, the same winds and the same streams rising but only one of them falls because the other one has listened to the words of the Master Builder and his house can stand firm in the midst of those storms.

Read the story of the Vine and the Branches found in John 15:1-17. This is a loaded passage with a list of important things to pick up on in this passage.

1. **What does the Father do to branches that don't bear fruit?**
   He cuts them off. He actually expects you to bear fruit.

2. **What does He do for branches that bear fruit? Why?**
   He prunes them so that you can bear even more fruit. Once vine branches grow out too far, it is hard for the vine to get enough nutrients through the branch to produce much fruit, and what it does produce typically isn't as good comparatively. Maybe you've seen someone who has started a business or ministry, and they get involved in too many things. This is an example of having your branches grow too far out. You're trying to have too big of a reach, but the problem is that you can't sustain it because you don't have enough nutrients going through at the time. You must be pruned in order to have that good fruit.

   An example in my life is when I was a financial advisor. One day I was sitting in my office and the Lord spoke to me and asked, "Justin, where have you seen the most fruit, the biggest fruit, the most long-lasting fruit, and where did it come the easiest? Is it in business or in ministry?" I knew the answer was in ministry. Then He said to me," Then you need to be pruned, and you need to stop doing business"

3. **What do we need to do in order to bear fruit?**
   To remain in the vine. This means remaining in the Lord and letting Him remain in you.

4. **Can we bear fruit on our own?**
   No. It says we can do nothing. Do you know that Paul tells us in **1 Corinthians 3:13-15** that each man's work will be tested by fire. He says, **"If what has been built survives, the builder will receive a reward. If it is burned up, the builder will suffer loss but yet will be saved—even though only as one escaping through the flames." (NIV)**

   Imagine that you had done all this work in your life, but it really wasn't about pointing people to Jesus, or that you had done it from selfish motives. We can end up still going to heaven, but yet our work itself will not survive. We will have nothing to show for how we loved the Lord during our lifetime. It will be as though we had done nothing at all.

5. **What brings the Father glory? (John 15:8)**
   That we bear much fruit!

6. **What does it show when we bear fruit?**
   It shows we are Jesus' disciples!

7. **How does Jesus love us?**
   Jesus loves us exactly like the Father loves Him!! What an incredible thought!

8. **What causes Jesus to call us His friends?**
   If we do what He commands. Obedience is also how He tells us to remain in His love. And it says it causes His joy to be in us and our joy to be full.

This is actually an important point because in the current culture, we like to push that Jesus is everybody's friend. But here He clearly says that you are His friend if you do what He says. His love is unconditional, but it isn't wise to make your friendships unconditional.

9. **How did Jesus learn what He knows?**
    He says that He learned it from the Father and made it known to us.

10. **What did Jesus appoint us to do?**
    Bear fruit-fruit that will last. And so that whatever we ask in His name the Father will give us. Wow!

11. **What is His command?**
    Love each other.

Now, whether you are discipling someone or being discipled, there is a good practice to have. It must become communal. It should never end up that one person becomes our source for all answers. Strength comes into discipleship as a community gathers because then I am never solely reliant on one person. It lets you know that the growth that is happening isn't just one person's efforts or thoughts, but it is about knowing Christ and His ways for life and living it to the fullest.

I encourage you to write down certain areas that you struggle with. Start with some actionable areas (i.e., health, finances, feeling closer to God, etc.). Then write down some mindsets that you need help with (i.e., my family struggles with health, rich people are greedy, I'm nobody special, etc.).

Now, concerning those areas, write down the names of some people you know and trust that have had the kind of fruit or success in those areas that you want to have?
1. **Contact them this week.**

2. Tell them you've noticed that they have done well in this part of life.
3. Tell them you are going through something.
4. Ask if they would be willing to give you some advice.
5. Some of this sounds hard to do, but humility goes a long way and people are more willing to help than you realize.
6. If you don't know anybody you feel comfortable sharing certain areas with, perhaps share that with the main person discipling you. They may have some experience in that area or know somebody who does.

CHAPTER 2

Keeping It All About Jesus

Praying The Scriptures

In this book, we cover a lot of different topics. Much of the reason why I have done my discipleship training the way I have is because it gives solid practices to go back to that keep me following Jesus with a healthy heart and mind. They are topics and practices that I would call spiritual sciences. I don't need to constantly guess how God wants things done, He gave them through His Son. I can know how He designed things to work. Because of that, even though life may not work out as I plan all the time, I can know how to use each part of it to grow closer to the Lord.

That is what I want to land on when all is said and done. There are so many things we can do simply because they are good practices. But the only way any of this matter is if we keep it all focused on Jesus.

Jesus corrected the Pharisees for thinking they would experience God's life or presence simply by knowing the Bible. He was saying, in essence, "You study the Bible, but you are not willing to come to Me in an ongoing conversation that you may experience God's presence."

You search the Scriptures, for in them you think you have eternal life; and these are they which testify of [point to] Me. But you are not willing to come to Me [talk to Me] that you may have life [experience God's presence]. (Jn. 5:39-40)

It isn't enough just to study the Word—we are meant to talk with God as we read it. Bible study is meant to create an active dialogue in our hearts with God. One way in which we gain strength in our prayer lives is by feeding on the Word through engaging in conversation with God as we read it.

There is a great difference between what I can remember in a lecture versus what I can remember from a dialogue where my emotions and an actual situation are engaged. Think of how many hours you spent in school. Now think about how many academic lessons you remember verbatim versus how many life lessons you remember from your parents or a coach, etc. With less hours spent, you remembered more because it was learned pertaining to an actual life situation and in dialogue instead of just lecture. Likewise, we are meant to read the scripture and have questions both about what the scripture is saying and what we are dealing with in life that pertains to that scripture.

Scripture gives us the conversational material for our prayer lives. Talking to God as we read the Word makes prayer easy and enjoyable. We speak the truths of the Word back to God as we read.

Moving from a pure study mode of the scripture to conversational mode was one of the greatest shifts in my spiritual life. It causes God's word to abide in you like is mentioned in **John 15:7**. This causes new desires to be formed in us and makes us be more sensitive to the Spirit's leading, including how to pray. It causes us to walk in more unity with God and prayer becomes much more enjoyable, but also more effective because we know it is deep in our heart and not just words that we think we should be saying.

There are two broad categories of Scripture related to pray-reading the Word—**promises to believe and exhortations to obey.**

With **promises to believe**, first, thank God for that truth, and second, ask the Spirit to give you more understanding of it. First, we thank God for a particular truth—turn it into a declaration of thanksgiving or trust.

For example, when reading that Jesus loves you as the Father loves Him, pray, "Thank You, Jesus, that You love me with the same intensity with which the Father loves You."
"As the Father loved Me, I also have loved you; abide in My love." John 15:9

Second, we ask God for more understanding of a specific truth. For example, while reading that Jesus loves you as the Father loves Him, pray, "Jesus, give me more understanding about how You love me with the same intensity with which the Father loves You."

With exhortations to obey, first, I commit myself to obey that truth, and second, I ask the Holy Spirit to help me. I don't just want to know what the Bible is saying intellectually, I want to walk closer to the Lord and watch the scriptures come to manifest in my life. I want to know them through experience.

Again, praying the scriptures allows us to really be taught by the Holy Spirit. Jesus said that the Spirit would remind us of everything that He had said. Then I want to make sure I have some things that the Lord has said somewhere in my mind for the Holy Spirit to remind me of. John reiterated this in his letters. **But the anointing which you have received from Him abides in you, and you do not need that anyone teach you; but as the same anointing teaches you concerning all things... (1 Jn. 2:27)**

Some last notes on praying the scriptures. Don't over-complicate it. When you see something in scripture, or are reminded of it, and you think things like you really want to see that in your life, or you need that, or you agree with the Lord, simply start having that conversation with Him. But I encourage being simple. Speak slowly and softly and use short phrases. You can simply say, "I need that, Lord," or, "I agree with You." It doesn't need to be long paragraphs.

Lastly, I would tell you that journaling goes a long way. And for people rolling their eyes right now, just like above, it doesn't need to be paragraphs. All you want to do is capture your conversations with the Lord. It can be saying, "I agree," and then the scripture reference. But it will help you develop language that you use to speak with God concerning His truth.

Keep the Greatest Command in First Place

What is our entire focus to be on? What did we do in the beginning with Him? We just want to walk and talk with Jesus and draw closer to Him.

Jesus said that the Greatest Commandment **(Matthew 22:37-38)** was to love the Lord with our heart, soul, and mind. And in **Ezekiel 36:27** it says that He would put His Spirit in us causing us to obey all of His decrees. What is the main thing the Holy Spirit causes us to do? Love God with our entire being!

People get hung up on the Holy Spirit being just about bearing the fruit or manifesting the spiritual gifts. Listen, you need God to love God! Without Him, it's impossible! We have to do it by His Spirit, by His power, according to His ways! But He calls loving Him the first and greatest commandment! It must be the first thought! And it must be the dominant thought!

Some have thrown this out and said the only thing we need to focus on now is to love our neighbor as ourselves. I am going to throw a whole lot of water on that! That is the second commandment. It is like it, not less, but it is second! Why? Because my love for God should cause me to obey Him! My love for my neighbor should not cause me to automatically obey them!

But there has been a huge move of the Church into social action. If it isn't focused on Jesus, and according to His ways, it will implode on itself! If love isn't defined the way Jesus does, it will not last! **And**

in the book of Revelation chapter 2, Jesus says to John concerning the church of Ephesus, "You have abandoned your first love. And either you return to it, or I will remove your lampstand." Essentially, "I will take away your ability to have light and give light to your city."

Loving the Lord must be our first priority, always. And that will always be the battle that the Enemy tries to wage with us. "Did the Lord really mean that? Did He really say that's the way life is supposed to work? Maybe a different way is better." But it's all a lie. It makes you feel better because other people accept you better, but you must stay where the Lord is.

Listen, the Apostles who had been with Jesus, loved Him so much and wanted to be back with Him. Therefore, they constantly talked about Him. Manifested His goodness on the earth. And their thought process was that if you were going to kill them, that was just fine because then they would be back with the One they loved.

Again, don't overcomplicate things. But we are called to love Him with all our heart, soul, and mind. It's really talking about our affections, our decisions, and our thoughts. If we are really focusing those things on Him, that's where "with all our strength" comes in. It should play out in our actions.

"Lord, I want to think about You all the time. My life isn't my own. I want to have your thoughts. I want to set my affection and emotions on what you have affections for and in ways that line up with Your heart. I want to exercise my will to make decisions like You make. And I want to see my life look more like Yours."

It's really that simple. But go after it. Go after Him. I am telling you right now that He is worthy, and He is worth it. Even the times that don't feel the greatest are worth it in the end. I am telling you that from experience. Get to know Him. And walk with Him.

CHAPTER 3

Joy and peace

Seek First The Kingdom

A lot of times we have a backward approach in the Church to how we make disciples. We tend to think that if we just give people the information, they will start acting the way that they should and eventually become part of us. But science tells us that if people feel like they belong then they will start believing the way we believe and then start acting the way we act. This is the way Jesus did it too. Jesus offered us joy, then invited us into His family, and told us what it looks like to be a part of His family.

We can see this through various scriptures. He gave us joy. **Acts 10:38 tells us that God anointed Jesus of Nazareth with the Holy Spirit and power, and that He went around doing good and healing all who were under the power of the devil, because God was with Him.**

He invited us into His Kingdom and Family. **John 1:12 says, "To those who received Him, to those who believed in His name, He gave the right to become children of God." And Matthew 12:46-50 says that those who do the will of His Father are His mother, brother, and sister. He even taught us in the Lord's prayer not just to pray "His Father" but "Our Father".**

And He taught us what His Family/Kingdom looked like. Most of the parables start with, **"The Kingdom of Heaven is like..."**

Paul tells us in Romans 14:17, "The Kingdom of Heaven is righteousness, peace, and joy in the Holy Spirit." This is amazing when we realize that Jesus told us in Matthew 6:33 to seek first the Kingdom of God and His righteousness. And then He tells us that all these things, the solutions to our needs, will be added to us.

We are told to seek first right standing with God, peace, and joy in the Holy Spirit and all our needs will be supplied. Do you know that science shows us this as well? Our bodies have a very hard time healing when they feel alone, stressed out, and depressed. But they tend to heal very well when they are connected to community and have peace and joy.

We tend to not get very good revelation when we are disconnected, stressed, or depressed. But we tend to get very good ideas when we are connected and have peace and joy.

Both this picture and the Beatitudes teach us how to have a good relationship with God and others, and that it will manifest the Kingdom into the earth. seek right relationship with God, seek peace and joy. Much of this not only gains relationship with others, but also favor and grace.

Without peace and joy, we will always be in survival, self-preservation mode. If I'm stressed out about paying my rent, I will feel the need to be greedy or steal. If a guy disrespects me, I will need to protect my self-worth. Our emotional and spiritual maturity largely stems from how well we can keep our joy and peace even in the midst of trials or threats. This is also why we are told to forgive and receive forgiveness. It frees us up to not dwell on the negative or stay in a victim mindset.

This is actually what Paul calls the difference between the carnal mind (flesh) and the spiritual mind. The carnal mind is always trying to figure out how to get its needs met rather than realizing it is taken care of. And this is where sin enters in.

True sin is not simply the acts we see people doing that we typically call sin. Those are the symptoms, but they are not the sickness. Jesus often showed frustration with unbelief and called it sin. Why? Because real sin is unbelief and has been growing inside of us for a while before we ever show outward manifestations. All sin starts with the unbelief that God is not who He says He is, we aren't who He says we are, and He doesn't care for us the way He says He will.

If I don't believe God is my Father, I will look for identity somewhere else. If I don't believe I am His good child, I will look for validation somewhere else. If I don't believe He will provide and protect me, then I will look for ways to do it myself.

Say that two people walk into a restaurant. Person A has all their bills taken care of, but person B is concerned that they won't be able to pay rent. As they pass a table, there is a sizable tip left for the waitress. Person B is far more likely to be tempted by taking the tip off the table because they have an unmet need. It's why we must stay in belief that God sees us and cares for us. If we stay in that place, the chances of even being tempted are greatly diminished.

So, without peace and joy, we are very likely to keep returning to this survival mode. It is very hard to live from a spiritual mind. We must recover places in our lives where we have lost peace and joy. I often ask people if they believe what they lost was for a season that they are supposed to let go and move on from or if it is something they feel they are supposed to recover. But often when someone is caught in these cycles, instead of helping recover

peace and joy, we add guilt and shame for the actions they did. In turn, this keeps them in the cycle.

Studies show that we are changed much more by who we are in relationship with, who brings us joy, than by what we believe. This is why Jesus tells us the Greatest Commandment is to love the Lord, your God, with all your heart, soul, mind, and strength. Because if He is where I get the most joy, then He is the one I will look like. But if I love my parents, friends, etc first, I will look like them. I will even carry around their bad habits and attitudes.

Other scriptures pertaining to peace and joy
1. **If it is possible, as far as it depends on you, live at peace with everyone. Romans 12:18**
2. **Peace I leave with you; my peace I give you. I do not give to you as the world gives. Do not let your hearts be troubled and do not be afraid. John 14:27**
3. **"This day is holy to our Lord. Do not grieve, for the joy of the LORD is your strength." Nehemiah 8:10**
4. **This is the day the LORD has made. We will rejoice and be glad in it. Psalm 118:24**
5. **Beloved, I pray that in every way you may prosper and enjoy good health, as your soul also prospers. 3 John 1:2**

Jesus invited us into His family. And His family is full of peace and joy. Our job as believers is actually very simple. We simply look for where people don't feel in right standing with God, where they have lack of peace, or where they have a lack of joy, and then we bring that to them.

The Joy of the Lord

In the Church, a lot of people like to talk about the presence of the Lord. But let's look at what Psalm 16:11 says about His presence. **"You make known to me the path of life; in Your presence there is fullness of joy; at Your right hand are pleasures forevermore." (ESV)** So according to scripture, being in God's presence there is fullness of joy. Being in God's presence fills us with joy! If you need more joy, you need to get into His presence more! And if you are spending time in prayer and come out with negative attitudes, you should question whose presence you were in.

The biggest agent of change in us is not what we say we believe. It is who we obtain the most joy from that determines how we think, believe, and act. I mentioned above that that is the reason for the Greatest Commandment, but it is also the reason why in **2 Peter 2:3-11** as Peter lists the order of how to build a productive faith, he mentions having brotherly love above having love for everyone. If we don't have a love for other believers first, we run the risk of becoming just like the world.

Another key factor in all of this is the Beatitudes, that the beginning of each one is "blessed is…" The term "blessed" can also be interpreted as "happy" or "joyful". We will dive deeper into this later, that being full of joy is one of the key traits of our people, but there is something interesting to ask about the beatitudes. How are some of these supposed to make us full of joy? It says that those who are poor in spirit, those who mourn, those who are persecuted are supposed to be full of joy. How can that be?

A key lies in knowing what joy really is. Joy is much deeper than happiness. You can be happy all by yourself, but Jim Wilder, a PhD in Theology and Neuroscience, makes a distinction in that joy is a "glad to be together" experience. This means that happiness may be experienced by one's self, but joy must involve more than one being.

Then how can we be full of joy while going through really hard times? When we know that every situation brings us into deeper relationship.

The Joy of the Cross

Hebrews 12:2 says, "For the joy set before Him He endured the cross, scorning its shame, and sat down at the right hand of the throne of God." (NIV) The way Jesus was able to go through the excruciating pain and humiliation of the cross was by looking to the joy that was set before Him. Do you know what that joy was? You and me. He wanted us in our unafraid, unashamed state able to have a relationship with Him. He also looked forward to pleasing the Father by bringing us back into Unity with Him.

Why did He despise the shame? For the first time He felt what sin was like. For the first time He experienced the shame that we had all carried, the fear we had of people finding out the wickedness that lay in us. However, instead of hiding like we do, He had prepared for this particular time to be hung out in front of everyone with nowhere to hide. And feeling that shame that we carried, He despised it. He despised that feeling of wanting to hide and never wanted us to feel it again.

Nehemiah 8:10 tells us, "This day is holy to our Lord. Do not grieve, for the joy of the LORD is your strength." (NIV) If we need more strength, we need more joy! But it's not just any joy, it's the joy of the Lord. So, what is His joy? It's pleasing the Father and having a relationship with us. This is critical because it isn't just us having joy in the Lord by our own idea of what that means. It's knowing that relationship with us brings Him joy.

Similar to how He said about Mary Magdalene when she poured perfume over him that whoever is forgiven much, loves much. If we want to love more, we need to realize how much we have been forgiven. The more we realize we are forgiven, the more we realize how much He simply desires relationship with us. The more we realize that and are filled with His love, we are able to love Him and others as well. We will only love to the extent that we know His love for us. How we treat others reveals how we believe God treats us.

In John 15:10-11 He says He tells us to keep His commandments of loving one another so that we stay in His love, and that staying in His love brings fullness of joy! That sounds a lot like Psalm 16!

Therefore, if we look, there is a cycle that is described.
1. **Being in His presence brings fullness of joy! (Psalm 16)**
2. **When we have more joy, we have more strength. (Nehemiah 8)**
3. **When we have more strength and joy, we live more like we should, even without focusing on it much of the time. We carry out His commandments which keeps us in His love (gives us a deeper sense of His presence). (John 15)**
4. **Staying in His love makes our joy full. (Repeat the process)**

Thank You, God! You let us come into Your presence. Remind us that You are our good Father, we are Your good children, and you love us beyond measure. Fill us with Your joy and give us strength to walk in Your ways. Then we can know we are staying in Your love and our joy and strength will increase all the more!

CHAPTER 4

Attachment

Hesed: Every Attachment Costs You Something

Remember that joy ultimately is a "glad to be with you" experience. We said there are multiple necessities in order for us to continually grow. We covered joy, but if it must be done in relation to another being, we need to discuss attachment.

Hesed (pronounced "heh-sed") is the Hebrew word for "attachment love". It is much more than simply a warm feeling, but it is the love that causes us to spur action for someone simply because they are part of a covenant community. Many Bible scholars believe that the Greek word "agape" used in the New Testament is trying to communicate what the word "hesed" means in Hebrew.

However, even by the way we translate it into English, there seems to be a deeper meaning to certain scriptures if they were written in Hebrew. Some of this is because of how easily we throw around the word "love". But the attachment love of "hesed" means that it is not a sacrifice for me to go into a burning building for you because if something happens to you, it happens to me. If life is hard for you, it's hard for me. This is much like how Paul tells us in **Romans 12:15** that we are to **"rejoice with those who rejoice and mourn with those who mourn."**
Imagine the scriptures reading more like, **"For God so attached Himself to the world that He gave His one and only son."** Or,

"Attach yourself to the Lord your God, and attach yourself to your neighbor as yourself." I don't know about you, but to me that feels like it carries more weight.

It sounds great to say that you're going to attach yourself to the Lord, but we need to talk about the practicalities of that.

It makes sense that everybody or everything you attach yourself to means that you can't attach yourself to someone else or something else, right? When you get married, you are saying, "I'm not seeing anybody else." When you take a job, it typically means you won't be doing any work for their competitors. There is a cost to attaching yourself to someone or something. When you are choosing to work, it means you are choosing not to do anything else during that time. If you have $100 and you decide to spend it on something, that means you can't spend it on anything else.

> **Luke 14:25-33 "Now great crowds accompanied him, and he turned and said to them, 'If anyone comes to me and does not hate his own father and mother and wife and children and brothers and sisters, yes, and even his own life, he cannot be my disciple. Whoever does not bear his own cross and come after me cannot be my disciple. For which of you, desiring to build a tower, does not first sit down and count the cost, whether he has enough to complete it? Otherwise, when he has laid a foundation and is not able to finish, all who see it begin to mock him, saying, "This man began to build and was not able to finish." Or what king, going out to encounter another king in war, will not sit down first and deliberate whether he is able with ten thousand to meet him who comes against him with twenty thousand? And if not, while the other is yet a great way off, he sends a delegation and asks for terms of peace. So therefore, any one of you who does not renounce all that he has cannot be my disciple." (ESV)**

What does this tell us, then, about how we are to love Jesus compared to everybody else? First, the word hate here is better translated as "to love less than". But your love for God should be so far ahead of your love for everybody else, that at times it may be taken as hatred. If God tells me to do something and a friend or family member advises me against it, I actually want to have a hatred for it if I even consider it. This is similar to when Peter told Jesus He would not go to the cross, and Jesus replied, "Get behind Me, Satan!"

But the other thing that is expressed here is that we need to count the cost ahead of time. If we wait until we are in tough situations to make up our mind, we will freeze. We need to take an account of if there are things we aren't willing to do. Sure, we say we are willing to go across the world for Jesus, but are we willing to make a fool of ourselves in our hometown? If it wouldn't just cost us our current job but possibly a lot of future jobs, would that make you question doing what the Lord told you? If we wait until the moment comes, we are likely to say things like, "Well, logically the Lord wouldn't want me to give up the ability to provide for my family." If you wait to count the cost, you will be tempted to say, "Maybe that scripture doesn't mean what it says because that offends my friend."

But these scriptures tell us that to not count the cost is much riskier. People will mock and say you couldn't continue with what you started. They will tell you, "See, it was fun to chase Jesus for a while, but it was just a fad." The hard part is that every time you deny Jesus trains your heart to do it again.

> **John 15:18, 19 "If the world hates you, know that it has hated Me before it hated you. If you were of the world, the world would love you as its own; but because you are not of the world, but I chose you out of the world, therefore the world hates you." (ESV)**

Because Jesus was hated first, we can expect people to hate us as well when we follow Him. A lot of this is because people have their own ideas in mind, rather than God's ideas. Their ideas are self-serving, but God looks to serve others.

> **Luke 9:23-27 "And he said to all, 'If anyone would come after Me, let him deny himself and take up his cross daily and follow Me. For whoever would save his life will lose it, but whoever loses his life for My sake will save it. For what does it profit a man if he gains the whole world and loses or forfeits himself? For whoever is ashamed of Me and of My words, of him will the Son of Man be ashamed when He comes in His glory and the glory of the Father and of the holy angels. But I tell you truly, there are some standing here who will not taste death until they see the kingdom of God.'" (ESV)**

This can seem like an extreme statement to make, but it really comes down to the basis of what we are talking about. Attachments cost you something. Am I going to be attached to Christ or the world? Am I going to be ashamed of my fleshly desires or of Christ? How often do we come to a point where we let our decisions slip because even though we know that God says one thing, we figure it might not be that big of a deal or that He will forgive us for it later. But every time we are doing that, we are training our heart to side with the world rather than to be like Christ and say, "Get behind Me, Satan. For you do not have the concerns of God in mind but the concerns of man." But Jesus says that if we are ashamed of Him, He will be ashamed of us when He returns.

> **Luke 9:57-62 As they were going along the road, someone said to him, "I will follow you wherever you go." And Jesus said to him, "Foxes have holes, and birds of the air have nests, but the Son of Man has nowhere to lay his head." To another he said, "Follow me." But he said, "Lord, let me first go and bury my father." And Jesus said to him, "Leave the dead to bury their own dead. But as for you, go and proclaim the kingdom of God." Yet another said, "I will follow you, Lord, but let me first say farewell to those at my home."**

Jesus said to him, "No one who puts his hand to the plow and looks back is fit for the kingdom of God." (ESV)

Here Jesus says that following Him can cost you in multiple ways. Many people think that Jesus was homeless as some sign of humility. But He most likely was not homeless. He most likely inherited the home that belonged to Joseph because we eventually don't hear about Joseph anymore. He also had been a carpenter for most of His life. Jesus isn't saying that everyone should get rid of their home.

But what He is saying is that it may cost you your ability to stay home and get away time, the things that make you look responsible, and your possessions. When we become believers, we are all called to ministry, and ministry costs you. He may put things on your heart and people may come looking for you for help. To the first guy He says there are no off hours. You don't get to clock out at 5pm. People will come to you at inconvenient times and ask for inconvenient things.

To the second He is saying there are certain responsibilities that if you put aside people may think you're uncaring or irresponsible. But it's that God knows best where you should be. Are you going to care more about what people think about you or about what God is telling you to do?

Lastly, He tells the follower that there are things you need to give up. Some people may think you are foolish for it, but if God tells you to give up property, He knows what He is doing. And He even told His disciples that anyone who gave up houses or family for His sake would receive one hundred times as much in this life and the next.

There is also a time where Jesus meets a rich young ruler. He tells the man he must sell all his possessions and give it to the poor if he wants to be perfect. This young man unfortunately cannot fulfill that, and it says that as he walked away sad Jesus looked at him and loved him. How is this love? Most of us would try chasing him down to soften the blow. But Jesus knew this guy simply could not be His follower. If you allow anything else a greater say in your life, you simply cannot follow Christ, not because He is being harsh, but because it is a fact that you will follow that thing or person instead of Him.

And as Jesus watched this man walk away, it was an act of love. It was grace and is for anyone else as well. If He would have allowed that man to follow Him, he would have felt judged constantly. When other disciples talked about how much they had given up to follow Jesus, he would have felt like they were judging him.

Take some time. Ask yourself what some costs are that you need to count. What are some things Jesus could possibly ask you to leave behind for Him? Are any of them difficult to think about giving up?

Trust me, this is not a one and done conversation. Years down the road we still find Jesus saying there are things to give up. When He leads us into new seasons, He often tells us we need to leave certain things behind or detach from certain people or ministries. It isn't because those things are bad but that they won't serve the purpose for the season He is taking us into. Will you continue to give Him first place?

Our Father-Jesus Was Always Inviting Us into His Family

Before we ever thought about attaching ourselves to Jesus, He attached Himself to us. John 1:11-13 says, "He came to his own, and His own people did not receive Him. But to all who did receive Him, who believed in His name, He gave the right to become children of God, who were born, not of blood nor of the will of the flesh nor of the will of man, but of God."

In Matthew 6:9-13 Jesus taught us to pray "Our Father." He didn't say "My Father". He hadn't even died yet. But if you received Jesus, He gave you the right to be a child of God.

According to Matthew 12:50, who did Jesus say are His brother, sister, or mother? Those who do the will of His Father. So being accepted into His Family isn't a matter of simply saying a prayer or saying you believe. You have to carry it out.

There was a cost for God attaching Himself to us like this. **"For God so loved the world, that he gave his only Son, that whoever believes in him should not perish but have eternal life." John 3:16 (NIV)**

According to Revelation 13:8, that price was paid for us even before the foundations of the world were laid. And **Ephesians 1:4 says, "Even before he made the world, God loved us and chose us in Christ to be holy and without fault in his eyes." (NLT)**

It isn't saying He chose certain people who would choose Christ, it's saying that He chose Christ to be the redeemer so that Christ would be the Way you could be completely known by the Father even after the Fall of Sin. If God does everything relationally, you have to think He didn't just create this world and decide to put people in it. It says that He loved you before He formed the world. Therefore, He made this world because He was thinking of you. And then He also made a way, even before you were made, before sin entered the world, before the world itself, He had already made a way to make sure you could come back to Him.

So, Jesus not only gave us peace and joy, but an invitation into His Family. If you receive Him, you are given the right to call God not just His Father, but your Father. This is a Family where we look like our Father and do His will on the earth.

Next, we will start discussing what our Family, what His Kingdom looks like.

CHAPTER 5

Group identity

The Fastest And Most Permanent Way For Us to Change

We covered peace and joy and without that we'll have a very tough time responding from anything other than survival mode therefore we must recover the places where we have lost peace and joy.

And we know that Jesus invited us back into his family into the family of God the scriptures tell us that to be children of God according to **John 1:12** we must receive Jesus as the Creator and Lord and according to **Romans 10:8-9** we must believe in Him as both Savior and Messiah it says we must believe in our heart and confess with our mouth. This is a confession of both living in heaven and earth. Heaven is in your heart and with our mouths we manifest that into the Earth. It is also a part of not being ashamed of Jesus.

None of our good works can do it and it can't be Jesus plus anything it has to be and can only be through Christ alone, but it produces good works in us. **Ephesians 2:8-10** tells us that it isn't works first, but that we are saved unto good works. **James 2:17** tells us that faith without works is dead or not really faith at all. That saying we don't really mean what we say we don't really believe and what we say we believe. And as I've mentioned before the kingdom when scripture talks about the kingdom it's talking about how God designed things to work before sin entered.

Now we're going to tie all of that together. God designed us in a way that we need to rely on relationship. our intellect cannot perceive reality on its own. In fact, there's a reason why joy is an experience that must take place inside of relationship, and that without relationship, many people slip easily into depression. What got us in trouble in the first place was eating from the Tree of knowledge of Good and Evil rather than the tree of life.

We need attachment love to make life really matter. **1 Corinthians 13:1-3 "If I speak in the tongues of men and of angels, but have not love, I am a noisy gong or a clanging cymbal. and if I have prophetic powers and understand all Mysteries and all knowledge, and if I have all faith, so as to remove mountains, but have not love, I am nothing. if I give away all I have, and if I deliver up my body to be burned, but have not love, I gain nothing."**

Matthew 22:37-40 "And he said to him, ' You shall love the Lord your God with all your heart and with all your soul and with all your mind this is the great and first commandment. And a second is like it: you shall love your neighbor as yourself. on these two commandments depend all the law and the prophets."'

John 10:11 - 13 "I am the good shepherd. the Good Shepherd lays down his life for the sheep. he who is a Hired Hand and not a shepherd, who does not own the sheep, sees the wolf coming and the leaves the sheep and fleas, and the Wolf snatches them and scatters them. he flees because he is a Hired Hand and cares nothing for the sheep."

The command to love God first and then your neighbor is the key to living a fulfilling life. people will do things for love that they won't do simply for a job or an acquaintance. But you'll run into a burning building for someone you're attached to, such as your child or spouse. Workers get tired but people who are doing things because of Love have enduring energy.

But we have to be careful who we attach ourselves to. **1 Corinthians 15:33 says, "Do not be deceived: 'Bad Company ruins good morals'". And Galatians 5:22-23 says, "But the Fruit of the Spirit is love, joy, peace, patience, kindness, goodness, faithfulness, gentleness, self-control semicolon against such things there is no law."**

God's command to have attachment love to him first and above all others is not a pride thing. He knows that we are most quickly and permanently shaped by who we are attached to. Psychology is showing us that above everything that we believe or say we believe, we are more shaped by who we get the most joy from. Therefore, when He tells us to love Him above all others it is in order that we look like Him. It is so that even though I love my parents, I don't pick up their bad habits, sins, or addictions because I am attached to God more than I am attached to them. This goes for all other people too.

In parenting there's often the phrase that more is caught than taught. The same is with discipleship, but it is strange that often all we are looking for is to give people knowledge. But even the apostles talked about how they came not just with words but with demonstration. We don't typically change simply because we have gotten new information, but we change much more quickly and much more permanently when we observe someone, we respect doing a behavior.

For example, if my parents had always treated customer service representatives horribly, I would likely treat customer service

representatives horribly, and it would probably be hard for me to change that habit. The quickest way for me to change that habit would be for me to observe someone I respect treating customer service representatives with kindness and respect. Then I could mimic their behavior because I had seen it.

The same thing happens in the story of Jacob where he is working for his uncle Laban. His uncle Laban changes the wages on him multiple times, but Jacob gets him to agree that any streaked or spotted sheep would be his for his wages. Therefore, Jacob starts taking branches and putting them in front of the sheep when they would go to get water. These branches would have streaks and spots on them, and then they would have streaked or spotted sheep. This is because our minds are very strong and what we see has a very strong effect on our thought process. Likewise, if I keep my eyes on someone else, even myself, I will become less than what Jesus meant me to be. My only hope is to learn to keep my eyes on Jesus.

Now in places that I don't know how to grow into, or that I'm not receiving revelation from Jesus, these are the places that I need to be discipled by another human that is physically on the Earth right now. That's why it's important to be discipled, and not simply to be taught, or get knowledge from books or videos. Every wise person who is successful has stories about their mentors and people they followed. Again, the difference is that we need to weigh what we see of other people, even our mentors, against what we find Jesus to look like in the Bible.

What is Group Identity?
Group identity is the expected behaviors, attitudes, and actions of a particular group. If you walked into the house of a military family, you would probably know quickly that they are a military family. Or if you walked into the house of a wrestling family, or a baseball family, or a music family, you would probably pick up quickly the interests

of that family and could deduce what their lives center around. You would not be surprised by certain behaviors or attitudes they had. You would have certain expectations of what their schedules were like.

The same is with the family of God. Jesus gave us many clear pictures of what the family of God, the Kingdom of God, looks like.

We find many of these in the Beatitudes and The Sermon on the Mount. We also find them in the parables.

My encouragement to everyone is that when you find Jesus saying something in his teachings you find where He carries this out somewhere else in the gospel. For instance, Jesus tells us that to be the greatest you must be the servant of all. Later we find Him washing the feet of His disciples, taking the position of the lowest servant in the house. Jesus also said that you couldn't follow Him and be His disciple unless you hated all others more than Him. This means that if I know God has told me to do something but a family member or friend or even my own desires tell me not to go do that thing, I should absolutely despise that I even considered not following the Lord. Later, when Peter tells Jesus that he will not go to the cross, Jesus tells Peter, "Get behind me Satan."

Now we're going to look at some of those teachings that Jesus gave through the Beatitudes and The Parables and what it looks like to be part of the family of God. What does our family look like? What are the attitudes we carry? How do we respond to situations?

Jesus Was the Very Image

We're going to start with the Beatitudes. And with both the Parables and the Beatitudes I'm going to slightly shorten things up from the way that I would normally talk about them. I encourage you to study the Parables and the Beatitudes with the attitude that this is what our family and our kingdom looks like.

The Beatitudes are found in Matthew chapter 5. The first thing I want you to carry into the Beatitudes is realizing that the main quality each of them has is that we are blessed. Each beatitude starts with "blessed are". Other terms for "blessed" can be "happy" or "joyful". I prefer joyful because I believe it gives us a fuller picture and pulls us back into that reality of all good things are found inside of relationship.

Poor In Spirit

It starts by telling us that the poor in spirit are blessed because they will receive the kingdom of God. Now again how can I be happy, joyful, or blessed if I'm poor in spirit? One of the answers to this is because then I inherit the Kingdom of God. Paul tells us that the kingdom of God is righteousness, peace, and joy in the Holy Spirit. So, what does this tell me?

To be poor in spirit means that I know that there is nothing within me that can possibly overcome my obstacles. Poor in spirit means that unless someone steps in on my behalf, I have no hope. Therefore, I am blessed to come to the understanding that I have no hope of attaining Heaven on my own. Only then can I truly believe in Jesus and the Holy Spirit.

Many people go through this life trying to do everything on their own willpower, believing that if they just grit through it more better things will come. They get exhausted and worn out but still don't find all the answers they were looking for. But in our family, we don't need to worry about this. because one of the keys to our identity, is that we are extremely joyful, we are extremely blessed, because when I'm poor in spirit I don't carry the weight of feeling I need to get myself into heaven or have the answers because I am in relationship with the one who created and rules Heaven and Earth and who has all the answers.

Those Who Mourn

Then it tells us that those who mourn are blessed because they will be comforted. Again, how can I be happy or joyful because I'm mourning? And again, the blessing is at very least twofold. One is simply that I will get my comfort. But what a lot of people miss in the scripture is the same as before, that the true blessing that leads to me being comforted is that when I don't feel the need to look strong and conceal my mourning, it pulls me into relationship both with God and others in the family of God so that I can be comforted.

Many people are walking through this life carrying weight that they don't need to carry. They refuse to let anyone know they are struggling. This keeps them from getting the relief they're truly seeking. But we are blessed in the family of Christ because as Paul says this is a family that rejoices with those who rejoice and mourns with those who mourn. Therefore, I know that when I'm struggling, I have God and many of his children who I can go to, pour out what is going on, and receive comfort. Again, the relationship is the true blessing that leads to the secondary blessing of comfort.

The Meek

The meek are blessed because they will inherit the earth. The first thing we need to address here is that meekness is not weakness. Meekness is a restrained strength. It is a strength that is held under voluntary control. A good example of this is when Jesus tells his disciples to take swords when they are going to the garden but then telling them later not to use them. Why would you tell somebody to bring a sword, but then reprimand them for using them? If they had not taken swords into the garden, the guards would believe that they surrendered simply because they had to. But Jesus also said that nobody takes His life but that He laid it down freely. And it's the same with us. Someone who is weak would have had no choice but to surrender, but someone who is meek is actually saying, "I could crush you if I wanted to, but I am not going to."

Refusing to get things in our own strength shows that we believe that it's an inheritance and not something that we need to work for. That shows that we actually have a relationship with the Father because children don't work for their inheritance, fathers do. Fathers have already done the work and leave the inheritance for their children.

In our family we are blessed to know that the Father has given us really good things, and He has been keeping them safe for us until we can grow into the maturity where we can hold on to our inheritance rather than destroying it or letting it destroy us. We see that He also did this with the Israelites back in the Old Testament. He told them that they could not take over the entire promised land at once because they didn't know how to take care of it and the wild animals would overrun it. So, He left it in the hands of their enemies who knew how to take care of it until they were mature enough and they would take it over piece by piece.

It is when we enter the family of God, then, that we realize we have a lot of power and a lot of Might, but also that we don't need to fight for our inheritance. We simply need to be faithful and mature. As we do our inheritance is handed over to us, and this is how the meek inherit the earth because when people see powerful people who could overrun them and take what they wanted but choose kindness and forgiveness, people hand more trust over to us.

Those Who Hunger and Thirst

Those who hunger and thirst for righteousness are blessed because they will be filled. When all you want is right standing with God and relationship you will get it and you will get it in abundance.

Just a short time later Jesus tells us to seek the kingdom of God first and His righteousness and all these other things will be added to us. He goes on to say if we ask it will be given if we seek, we will find and if we knock the door will be open and he actually is saying to keep asking keep seeking and keep knocking. What does that mean? It means if you have a desire that you ask for it and keep asking until you have an idea of how it is to be done. Then you seek that out until you find opportunities. Once you find opportunities, you knock on those doors until one of them opens because Jesus then says that we know how to give good gifts even though we are evil fathers. Therefore, the Father knows much more how to give good things to anyone who asks. The problem is that many people stop after they ask, or they get an idea but do not pursue it. Jesus is telling us that we need to be people that pursue until the end. But the blessing for us is that we have a Father that desires to give us good gifts, and He desires us to be part of the process and part of our maturing as well as we pursue those good gifts.

The great part about what Jesus is saying is that you don't have to be concerned with actually even finding the kingdom or finding righteousness. He knows that if He told us we had to find heaven first, or find righteousness, that we would stress out, which would completely keep us from finding that Kingdom of righteousness, peace, and joy in the Holy Spirit. Instead, He tells us that we simply need to hunger for it and seek it and trust that we are in relationship with the One who gives really good gifts. Again, the blessing of our family is that everything drives us into deeper relationship.

The Merciful
The merciful are blessed because they will be shown mercy. **Matthew 6:14-15** says that if we forgive others God will forgive us but that if we don't forgive others we will not be forgiven. A lot of this doesn't have to do with the Father's willingness to forgive us but more so with our slowness to receive. It's like the scripture telling us that we will be judged according to how we judge. In the same way, if you don't have mercy, it will be hard for you to believe that you have been given mercy because you will believe in actions deserving judgment more than in God's desire to extend grace and forgiveness.

When it comes down to it, we treat people the way we believe God treats us. Therefore, if we treat others harshly, we believe that He judges us that way. But if we show mercy, it instills in us that it is because our Father is merciful. So, when I myself stumble, I don't doubt and shrink back from the Father because I know that I have extended mercy and that I am not better than He is. Extending mercy allows me to live a peace-filled life knowing that I'm in deep relationship with the Father.

Peacemakers
The peacemakers will be called sons of God. This goes all the way back to our conversations about the garden. We were put into the world that already had the enemy in it. We were created to manifest the kingdom into the earth. **Romans 14:17 "For the kingdom of God is not a matter of eating and drinking but of righteousness and peace and joy in the Holy spirit."**

Remember the first beatitude said that we inherit the Kingdom. This means we have peace as part of our inheritance. Notice people who have been true advocates for peace such as Martin Luther King, Jr. With all the negative things that the world likes to say about Christianity, people don't seem to have an issue with the fact that Martin Luther King, Jr. was a minister. Why? He ushered peace. When people bring peace, the world truly believes they were sent by God.

This isn't about being a peacekeeper. Peacekeepers often keep silent when things are bad because they just want to keep the peace. People who just want to keep the peace typically don't keep any peace; they are being filled with pride at believing nobody gets mad at them. But what they are allowing to happen is for disunity to slowly build as long as it is not manifested for a time. But eventually that disunity will erupt. Peacemakers, on the other hand, create peace where there is no peace and in doing so cause people to truly believe that their children of God.

Persecuted for Righteousness

Lastly, Jesus says that **those who are persecuted for righteousness** own the kingdom. **Matthew 5:10** This isn't just talking about being persecuted for "Being a Christian." I have had times where people are jerks, but say it is in the name of Jesus. Or they want to talk about Jesus at work, but not do the job they are being paid for. When they get talked to about their attitude, they say they are being persecuted for being a Christian, but that's not the case. It's because they wanted to be rude or lazy but use the name of Jesus for it.

This is talking about for righteousness' sake. That means when people try to persecute you because you are carrying out the characteristics of God. Many times, the terms "righteousness" and "godliness" are interchanged depending on the translation of the Bible you are reading. Even Christ Himself was persecuted. And He told us that if they hate us, it's because they hated Him first. They hated Him, so they hate the message you carry about Him.

When we can maintain our righteousness (or godliness), peace and joy in the midst of this, we have a deeper sense that we won't just inherit the Kingdom, but that we have inherited it. We have inherited looking like our Father Who was in the Son reconciling the world which was crucifying Him to Himself. We have inherited peace that goes beyond understanding and joy that is inexpressible. A good picture of this is Stephen who was able to present the Gospel even while being martyred. It is not just our Father's Kingdom at this point; Jesus says the Kingdom is ours.

Be careful that you don't let this lead you into a pompous way of thinking. Taking ownership is both about the benefits you get but also the responsibilities you have. Once you know what peace, joy, and righteousness look and feel like, it is your responsibility to stay in the place that you know God has given you grace for this. Your job is to refuse the heavy burden and the hard yoke to take up Jesus' which is light and easy.

But this is a huge place to come to. To know that you cannot be moved. That you are part of an unshakeable kingdom. Those who have their reputations ruined have a great heavenly reward. Jesus was persecuted on the cross, but then they made fun of Him while whipping Him, while nailing Him to the cross. What is our reward for this endurance? Knowing Jesus' heart more and loving people better.

"But lay up for yourselves treasures in heaven, where neither moth nor rust destroys and where thieves do not break in and steal." Matthew 6:20

"The master commended the dishonest manager for his shrewdness. For the sons of this world are more shrewd in dealing with their own generation than the sons of light." Luke 16:8 What is being said here is that people of this world know how to make sure there is wealth lined up for them in the future, or how to gain favor with people for future use. Likewise, we should be like this. The reward we get in heaven is seeing the people we came in contact with in life, also be in heaven.

Even while being persecuted, we want to be in a place of reconciliation and forgiveness so we can gain reward in heaven. Like Jesus on the cross: "Forgive them, for they don't know what they are doing." Or Stephen being stoned. Saul, who became Paul, was watching someone live in what he had been taught to chase his entire life. Eventually, Paul entered heaven to Stephen greeting him. Paul was part of Stephen's reward.

One more time, notice all of them say you are blessed. Blessed also means happy. Our family is really happy. Why? **Because**

everything in here pulls us into a greater relationship with the Father and with each other. It echoes what Jesus said are the Greatest Commandments:
a.   Love God
b.   Love each other

Our Family is really blessed. There is nothing that doesn't cause us to have greater relationship.

CHAPTER 6

The Parables of Jesus from Matthew and Mark

Again, we are looking at our group identity, but now we are going to move from looking at the Beatitudes to the Parables. As we do, we want to get the overall picture that Jesus was giving us, and some of the reasons why it is important. But we don't want to get caught up in analyzing it rather than simply absorbing the picture.

The Parables were a great delivery system for Jesus to use for a couple of reasons. One was that those who weren't ready to receive Jesus' teachings would simply think He was telling stories about farmers and fishermen. But the other is that instead of getting extremely analytical, Jesus used the stories to be an ongoing source of revelation. He gave us simple pictures that allow the Holy Spirit to continue using those pictures to give us more revelation as it comes back into our memory each time. We are just going to give basic touches on each of these and core concepts to our group identity. But know that the Holy Spirit will use these pictures to teach you other concepts as you keep walking with Him.

The Lamp - Matthew 5:14-16, Mark 4:21-25
James tells us that faith without works is dead. Jesus is using this picture of the lamp to tell us that we cannot hide our faith. People will see it. When people tell you that you should carry out your faith quietly, I would tell you that's impossible or it is no real faith at all.

There can be the temptation for some to look at those carrying out their faith and cry, "Self-righteous!" But Jesus says that it brings glory to the Father. It doesn't mean you should post tons of videos on Facebook about it, it means your faith should be so evident through action that people cannot deny you are a child of God!

The Speck and The Log - Matthew 7:1-5

It is a common talking point against anyone trying to hold accountability to use this scripture. However, this picture is not saying that we are never to judge. The point is to be aware of the plank in our own eye first. If we aren't removing that plank out of our own eye, we can't see clearly to help another remove the speck in theirs. And the truth is, you are probably only concerned about the speck in theirs because you see a small part of your own issues in them.

This isn't Jesus saying never to have discernment or accountability, but it is saying to be aware of your own log and not be a hypocrite.

The measure you judge with will come back to you for many reasons. One is simply that the way people watch you judge others is the same way they will respond to you. But also, that the way you judge others is a reflection of how you feel God is judging you.

New Cloth on Old Garment - Matthew 9:16-17, Mark 2:21-22

If you put a new cloth onto an old garment, if it is washed, it will shrink and pull away. The old and the new have to be separate. We can't try to live this New Covenant by trying to figure out how we are to combine it with the Old Covenant. The Law was there to show us that we cannot keep God's perfect Law. Mercy covers us if we do sin. In John's letters he says, **"My dear children, I write this to you so that you will not sin. But if anybody does sin, we have an advocate with the Father—Jesus Christ, the Righteous One. He is the atoning sacrifice for our sins, and not only for ours but also for the sins of the whole world." 1 John 2:1-2**

We also have grace that calls us into a higher place of living. The Law never made anyone perfect but only showed us we were imperfect. But the grace of the cross of Jesus has cleansed us and called us higher. Paul says the Law is actually for law breakers. Those who don't have a heart to break the law don't need a law to tell them how to act. Again, the scriptures tell us that the law is actually written on our hearts. But we are called to a new commandment, love one another.

Trying to reconcile the Old and New Covenant is a fruitless task. You will only find yourself being torn apart because you will want to believe in the grace of God but at the same time judging yourself for every wrong thing you've done. It makes people become useless in the Kingdom because it makes them self-focused instead of God focused. The biggest takeaway I can give you is that whether it is the Old or the New it is all to point to Jesus!

The Divided Kingdom - Matthew 12:24-30, Mark 3:23-27
This is actually very simple. It should make you wonder a little bit why much of the world seems to be just fine with every other religion but has issues with Christianity. But as for the Church, I would tell you to take a look at **Psalm 133** and look at what God has to say about people living in unity under Him. It looks a lot like **Acts 2:42-47**! Go read that and tell me you don't want to be a part of a church that looks like that!

The Sower - Matthew 13:1-23, Mark 4:1-20
Realize that there are 4 different types of soil, and Jesus says the message of the Kingdom is the seed. What determines what happens to the seed? The condition of the soil, the condition of your heart. The Proverbs tell us to guard our heart because out of it comes the wellspring of life. Much of the time, if we watch our heart, other things will fall into place: our minds won't be so anxious, our emotions will be more controlled, and our language will be much more Kingdom-filled.

If we want the Kingdom to grow in us, it is very important that we make sure our soil is taken care of properly. This is why we started this process by talking about Joy and Attachment and are now talking about Group Identity, because they are 3 out of the 4 main ingredients to ensure healthy soil.

The Growing Seed - Mark 4:26-29
This largely goes along with the last parable. We don't need to

stress out about growth and maturity in us or others. We just need to plant, water, fertilize, etc. The Kingdom will grow in us.

Parables of Growth
- **The Weeds Among the Wheat - Matthew 13:24-30**
- **The Mustard Seed - Matthew 13:31-32, Mark 4:30-34**
- **The Leaven - Matthew 13:33-34**

Key takeaways:
The enemy came and planted bad among the good. Don't worry about it. It will get taken care of.
The Kingdom will grow and grow. It starts off small in your heart, but it will grow. And just like the Mustard Seed, it will become so big that others will come to you for the Kingdom that you carry.

Parables of God's Heart for the World
- **Hidden Treasure - Matthew 13:44**
- **Pearl of Great Price - Matthew 13:45-46**
- **The Net - Matthew 13:47-50**
- **The Heart of Man - Matthew 15:10-20**
- **The Lost Sheep - Matthew 18:10-14**

Key takeaways:
Jesus gave a great price for the world. He saw the treasure in you when what most saw was the dirt. He sold everything He had, became poor so that we might become rich, in order to buy the entire field. He bought you dirt and all, not just the treasure.

This can also be turned around in that to gain the Kingdom, it does cost you. Think about even wanting to start a business and having freedom in finances and time. It would cost you something. You can't hang around the friends that just want to chill out. You will have to first give your time and your money in order to reach your desired goal of having financial freedom and time.
Again, Jesus reiterates, don't worry about the bad. He has that sorted out. And He adds to it not to look necessarily at external things, but to realize what comes out of a man.

Parables of Our Responsibility in the Kingdom
- **The Unforgiving Servant - Matthew 18:23-35**
- **Laborers in the Vineyard - Matthew 20:1-16**
- **The Two Sons - Matthew 21:28-32**

Key takeaways:
Jesus paid the price for us. And even if you were the only lost one in the world, He would have paid the same price to get you back because you are that important to Him.

You cannot be forgiven if you carry unforgiveness around in your heart.

There is a sense that we all get the same reward. Nobody gets more access to Jesus just because they have walked with Him longer. The success of the brother isn't in the verbal yes or no. It's when you carry out the will of our Father.

Parables of Maturing, Unity with God, and Judgment
- **The Tenant Farmers - Matthew 21:33-45**
- **Marriage Feast or Great Banquet - Matthew 22:1-14**
- **The Budding Fig Tree - Matthew 24:32-35, Mark 13:28-33**
- **The Faithful vs. The Wicked Servant - Matthew 24:45-51, Mark 13:34-37**
- **The Ten Virgins - Matthew 25:1-13**
- **Ten Talents or Gold Coins - Matthew 25:14-30**

Key takeaways:
These get down to what the end goal has always been. The cross wasn't the end goal, but we could never get there if it wasn't for the cross.

To walk in relationship with God means to be faithful in what He has given us.

He doesn't say the one servant is wise, and He doesn't just call him lazy. He calls him wicked as well. Faithfulness is attached to multiplication.

The oil in the lamps represents the anointing of the Holy Spirit. You can't get it from someone else. You have to get it yourself.

CHAPTER 7

The Parables of Jesus from Luke

Reading the Gospels can be a lot of fun because it is four different men telling what they knew of Jesus from four different perspectives. Out of them, the ones known for their parables are Matthew, Mark, and Luke. And out of those three, Matthew and Mark share many of the same ones while Luke has many completely different parables.

This is one of the places many critics of the scriptures think they have an argument, but it is much like four people giving eyewitness to any other account. There will be differences based on what is important to them, the message they are trying to convey, and the people to whom they are speaking.

Matthew, Mark, and John were disciples of Jesus giving account many years later after they had been able to test, see, and mature the lessons they had been taught. Luke, however, was a Greek who was working for Theophilus to be a historian and find out exactly who this Jesus was and what this new group of people belonging to "the Way" was. Luke also wrote the book of Acts. And in being a historian, one thing that Luke doesn't miss out on is details.

Where the last chapter had the Parables from Matthew and Mark, this chapter is going to look at what Luke had found.

Parables of Jesus Uniting Jew and Gentile
- **The Good Samaritan - Luke 10:29-37**
- **The Pharisee and The Tax Collector - Luke 18:9-14**

Key takeaways:
We have talked about attachment in this class. How the attachment love of God makes us not see sacrificing for another as a problem. If you are struggling in life, I'm struggling. If you're doing well, I rejoice with you. What was the Good Samaritan willing to do to take care of the victim in this parable? He took care of the man's needs, ensured his ongoing care, and promised to settle future needs.

The first guys to pass by in the Good Samaritan were religious leaders. What do we see about truly loving God in the Good Samaritan? It is interconnected with loving other human beings because they are made in His image. It doesn't matter what you think you've learned and can regurgitate. What matters is faith being expressed in love.

How about in the Pharisee and the Tax Collector? What did the Pharisee look at, and what did the Tax Collector look at? The Pharisee looked at his efforts to look good, but the Tax Collector was trusting God's mercy to make him right.

Parables About Praying and Not Giving Up
- **The Friend at Midnight - Luke 11:5-13**
- **The Persistent Widow - Luke 18:1-8**

Key takeaways:
Jesus is using this story to build in us a character of someone who will not give up. God will sometimes have us wait and keep asking, seeking, and knocking because He is more interested in who we are becoming than just us being able to have a one-time breakthrough.

For example, would He rather help us lift 300 pounds and be able to tell the story or help us become someone who can lift 300 pounds all the time? David trained by killing lions and bears. He was able to kill Goliath.

Parables on True Life Wisdom

- **The Rich Fool - Luke 12:13-21**
- **The Rich Man and Lazarus - Luke 16:19-31**

Key Takeaways:
What do you pick up about what our people value from these stories?

Christ followers tend to value eternal over temporal gain. It doesn't mean you can't get wealth, but we don't sacrifice the eternal for the momentary things.

Parables About God's Patience
- **The Barren Fig Tree - Luke 13:6-9**
- **The Invited Guests - Luke 14:7-14**

Key Takeaways:
What should you see about God's mercy and grace from this? He gives time after time. Jesus desires for there to be time to turn.

All of humanity has been invited into the Kingdom. First it was for a specific people group, but Christ made it an invitation to all. The downfall of most is that they value other things over coming in and being made full by eating and dwelling with God. They have a hard time giving it up.

The Father Spares Nothing to Seek You Out
- **The Lost Coin - Luke 15:8-10**
- **The Prodigal Son - Luke 15:11-32**

Key Takeaways:
In the parable of the Lost Coin, it can be attributed to Jesus

searching for us as a Lost Coin, but it can also be us seeking the Kingdom as a Lost Coin.

When you read the Prodigal Son, notice how the Father ran to the son before he could even get home.

1. He was always looking and ready for the son to return.
    1. I want you to know that from day one, He put His robe on you (you look like Him), He put His sandals on your feet (you walk like Him), He put His ring on your finger (you carry His authority), and He gave you a staff (you have His power). This isn't something you need to gain over time. It is yours from day one.
2. The speech the son had prepared didn't even matter. The Father's joy was to have His son back.
3. The older son had a pity party. The Father didn't tell him he had to leave for having a bad attitude. In fact, he also spoke to him as a Father.
    1. The older son had worked as a hired hand instead of knowing he was a son. He worked for everything he had and didn't ask for anything in return.
    2. What was the Father's response? "You've always been with Me and all I have is yours.
    3. What does this tell us about people with bad attitudes in the Church? God is their Father too and He loves them. They have probably seen it as though they need to work for God, but they don't realize they are a son. They think they need to work for everything and are upset with anyone they see receiving grace or recognition.
    4. What would have happened if the older brother would have realized he didn't have to be a hired hand? He probably would have hung out with his Father more. He would have heard his Father tell him he was a loved son. He also probably would have heard that the Father missed his brother. And if he loved his Father, he probably would have gone out to find his brother. If he would have gone to find his brother, do you think the Father would have given

Justin Heckel

him not only what he needed for the journey but also some things he wanted?

This wraps up our parables. But again, I want you to really grasp that this is who we are. This is what our Family and Kingdom look like. And as you keep these pictures in your heart and mind, the Holy Spirit will continue to give revelation concerning their meaning, our identity as believers, and paths you should take.

1. How do you feel your understanding of being part of the Kingdom is?
2. Do you feel the Father's love for you?
3. Do you know that if you run out He will run to get you back?
4. Do you know that He gives you everything you need for life and to live the Gospel?
5. I want to give you a picture that the Kingdom of righteousness, peace, and joy is sneaking onto you as if you were a child who put on his dad's clothes and are starting to grow into where they fit right.

CHAPTER 8

The New Creation

The last couple of chapters hammered on the parables and teachings where Christ was really giving us our group identity. There's one last part I want to touch on and then we are going to learn a little about ourselves as individuals.

Paul and the other Apostles Gave us a lot of group identity too. There were some important shifts that took place after the cross. Jesus highlighted them in John Chapters 14-16 when He told His disciples about the Holy Spirit coming. He did it again in the Great Commission when He said...

"Whoever believes and is baptized will be saved, but whoever does not believe will be condemned. And these signs will accompany those who believe: In my name they will drive out demons; they will speak in new tongues; they will pick up snakes with their hands; and when they drink deadly poison, it will not hurt them at all; they will place their hands on sick people, and they will get well."
Mark 16:16-18 (NIV)

Clearly, this is also for us today. It was not just for the Apostles. Because they already were doing those things. And He said they would go tell others, and those who believed would do these things.

He also told His disciples before ascending that they would receive the Holy Spirit. That is part of our new identity.

"Do not leave Jerusalem, but wait for the gift my Father promised, which you have heard me speak about. For John was baptized with water, but in a few days you will be baptized with the Holy Spirit."
Acts 1:4, 5 (NIV)

"But you will receive power when the Holy Spirit comes on you; and you will be my witnesses in Jerusalem, and in all Judea and Samaria, and to the ends of the earth."
Acts 1:8 (NIV)

The bottom line is this... **Believers are to carry the Holy Spirit. And the New Creation is to be completely different from the Old.** Remember the parable of the wine skins? To hold the new, we must be new. **The New Creation doesn't do things out of their own strength, but by relying on the Holy Spirit.** This is true for right living, for power, and for learning.

When we look at the need for the Holy Spirit and reliance on Him, it is mindblowing. Remember that Jesus said when He went away the Father would send another like Him. The word He used for "like" means "exactly like". It's the same as saying that Jesus was "exactly like" or the "very representation" of the Father. It accents the oneness of the Trinity.

But what does this mean for us? Well, it means that not only does He carry all the same attributes as Jesus but also that we are able to speak with the Holy Spirit just like the disciples were able to speak to Jesus. When the disciples would ask a question, I don't ever get the feeling that He made them feel ignored or that they would need to go fast for a month in order to get an answer. He may not have answered their question directly, but they always felt heard and given direction.

There is a need for the Holy Spirit to be both upon you and within you. The disciples already had Him on them for healing and casting out demons, but Jesus said He would be in them as they waited for that day of Pentecost. What does this mean?

As Bill Johnson says, "The Holy Spirit is in you for your sake and upon you for the sake of others." We need to carry Him on us just like the disciples so there is the belief in our ability to heal them (really the Holy Spirit healing them through us). It opens our ability to serve others.

On the flip side, we need the Holy Spirit in us for righteousness, peace, and joy. This is for our sake. It keeps us from letting our thoughts or emotions run wild and run the show. He is our teacher and gives us boldness.

Where the disciples were able to heal and cast out demons because of having the Holy Spirit on them, Peter still cowered when a girl asked him if he was a follower of Jesus. But after the Holy Spirit was in him, he was able to proclaim the Gospel to a crowd of thousands on the day of Pentecost. **We need Him in us and upon us.**

Part of the New Creation is knowing we are the Righteousness of God in Jesus Christ. We are in right standing with God because of Jesus, not our acts. But our acts are proof that we are in right standing.

As the New Creation, we understand our words have power. We must control our tongues. We have our Father's image in us, and He made the world through words. We do all the things laid out in the Great Commission and more. Jesus said we will do greater things than we saw Him do. Philip got translated from one place to another. We work in the impossible.

Through the Holy Spirit, our emotions are leveled instead of a roller coaster.

1. This is because we allow Him to heal us from our past.
2. We allow Him to teach us about our present.
3. We allow Him to inform us of our future.
4. This also keeps us from sinning because if I know my needs are taken care of, and I trust my Father to take care of them, I really don't have as much temptation in my life.

Basically, I can either be the old creation and a sinner, or I can be the New Creation, the righteousness of God, a saint. But I can't be both.

The last thing I want to bring up to you in all of this, is that everyone has a seat at the table. God made each person for a reason. It doesn't matter what they've come from, there is an image of God in them that they've let get covered up with dirt just as we all have, but God wants it redeemed. They have something valuable for the Kingdom.

CHAPTER 9

Finding Your Place

In the last chapter we discussed being a New Creation, the Righteousness of God in Jesus Christ, a Saint. **The Greek word used for "New" there is the same word we get "Prototype" from. You are something the world hasn't seen yet.**

When you do Strengthfinders and you pay to get all 52 strengths ranked in order, they tell you the math on percentages of people having the same top ten as you, percentages for having those top ten in the same order. When you break down the chances of how many people have the same 52 in the same order as you, the percentages are very small that not only is there nobody in the world like you, but there has also never been anybody in the world like you and there never will be.

As the New Creation we have the ability to work in the Holy Spirit to accomplish the work of Jesus Christ on the earth. The fruit of the Spirit shows our character and comes through maturity. However, things like healing don't simply happen through the fruit, that is a gift.

The gifts of the Spirit are gifts that are simply given. They can be used immaturely. But they are necessary for putting our ability to serve on an even playing field. Some churches have been very gifted but still tore each other apart and separated because they didn't grow the fruit of the Spirit.

We don't have a sin nature anymore; we have a God nature. How we act and the way we respond to our actions shows which nature we have and are aware of. To sin doesn't necessarily mean we have a sin nature. I can swim just fine and go underwater just fine, but to be under too long is going to really bother me. Because I don't have a fish nature. **Sin bothers me because it isn't my nature. To serve others brings me joy because it's in my new nature.**

We covered that everybody has a place in this New Creation. Or rather, everybody is invited to have a place, and they were created to have a place. The Old Creation didn't have a place for everyone. It was ruled by those with money, power, etc. In this one, everyone is valued because we know there is the image of God in them, and when the gold is found rather than just the dirt, when they are put into a place where they shine, we see what they were made for. That place may not look amazing to others. But those who know see that person and know this is where they are full of joy and are doing something they were specifically made for.

The first martyr was Stephen who was serving tables. People could have looked at him and weighed him against what they saw Peter doing, but this was where Stephen shined! It says that as he was taking care of these widows, he was working in such power it raised the Jews to jealousy and it caused them to stone him. The entire time he was being stoned, he was having visions of Jesus and proclaiming the Gospel. That day, Saul was there.

Imagine being Saul, later called Paul. You have worked your tail off to be the best Pharisee there is, to prove that you are closer to God than anyone could be. But as you're standing there watching this man be killed, he is in complete ecstasy and saying he sees the Lord. He is living in everything you have worked for! It had to mess with Saul's heart and mind. And he was standing too close to someone who carried the Spirit of God. Later, on the road to Damascus, he would meet Jesus in a radical way. **But it all started with a man who was simply working supernaturally in the place he was called to.**

It's important to realize that you don't need to try to be everyone. God has given you special gifts and abilities. It doesn't mean that you never need to grow, but the more you know who you are and what you are called to, the better you are at being able to determine what you should say yes to and what you should say no to. And that helps you not take on guilt and shame about situations in which you don't need to take it on. For example, I can do some handyman activities, but I'm not going to take on guilt or shame if I tell someone I can't help them install plumbing because I'm not a plumber.

I have 4 questions that help you find your place. I'm going to be honest and say that I have had a tough time with the way life coaches sometimes ask these kinds of questions. For some reason or another they don't always click with me the right way and make me think that it's sometimes true and sometimes not. I'm not saying they are wrong; I am saying there is more than one method and different methods work for different people. The Lord has known my heart and has known that I often need some very straight common sense for me to understand. Here are the questions:

1. What do you think needs to increase or decrease?
Isaiah 58:8 says, "Your righteousness (or godliness depending on the translation) will lead you forward, and the glory of the Lord will protect you from behind." The way I look at the word "righteousness" is "I am one with God, He is one with me, and He reveals Himself through me."

When I think, "God wouldn't want that to continue," or, "God would want that to increase," I don't have the luxury of not putting my hands to work. The Lord is revealing His desire to me and as being one with Him, I need to put action to that.

One rule we've had in our home for years now is that you don't get to simply say you hurt someone, or you just love them so much while they are going through something. Love looks like something. The rule in our house is that if you say you hurt for someone, you need to do whatever you can about it.

You need to manifest the fact that the Lord wants to reveal His character through you. The scripture says it leads you forward. And when you manifest it, the glory, or manifested goodness, of the Lord also protects you from behind.

This comes much easier by knowing your people and your community. People are always searching for their purpose. If you find your people, finding your purpose is much easier. It's hard to think about what you should do or who you should be when you look at the whole world. But being able to see ways to help your community is much easier.

What do you think needs to increase or decrease? What are issues that really bother you or things you wish your community would do a better job at? It may be what the Lord is calling you to.

2. What do people come to you for?
Many times, people ask what you're gifted in, but we often aren't aware of what our gifts are because it's normal to us. David killed bears for a long time before fighting Goliath. It was normal.

Do people come to you for relationship advice? To help build businesses? To work on cars or houses? Knowledge? They come to you because it isn't a gift they carry, but it is one you possess. And gifts are for giving.

3. Who do you hear speak and you hear your voice?
There are a lot of people with platforms out there, either in public speaking or on social media. Maybe there's somebody in your community. Some people have dad's that they know they need to

keep a specific family trait going because when they start talking, they feel their dad's voice coming out.

There are a lot of people on social media that say things similar to me regarding interests I have. However, I can tell we have a different energy or passion about the topic.

But then there are certain people, especially those in ministry that I hear them speak and I realize they are just like me. Maybe they are even a few steps ahead of me. It doesn't mean that I mimic them, but I can use it as a gauge for helping me find my bearings. Sometimes I realize I really want to run alongside that person as well.

4. What direction do you head and receive resistance? (Fear, mocking, etc.)

Life has been set up in such a way that any time you are pushing in an upward trajectory concerning an area of life, you will receive pushback.

If you went from working at McDonald's to doing missions overseas, I guarantee there would be doubts creeping in. "How do I get funding? People think I'm crazy. What if it's too dangerous over there?" However, if you reversed that and quit missions to come back to America and work at McDonald's, you would probably receive zero resistance.

Have you tried to start a ministry or business and heard, "There's no way you're going to make that work"? Or maybe you've tried to pursue a degree and you're reminded that studying has never been your strong suit or that it will cost a lot of money.

This is the way God has designed life to ask you if you really want this at this time. If you're really called to start that business but then you back down when the first hard season starts, let me tell you that you will eventually want to return to the business. Your heart is what dictates your desires, not your mind. But your mind has a lot of ability to cast doubts. That's why part of the prophetic is to confirm and affirm what is on our hearts.

You'll hear people say things like, "The enemy is attacking me because they don't want me starting this business." Well, in a sense that's true. He's feeding you lies. However, this is again a design of the Lord that this is where the enemy is allowed to confront you, so you are put in a position to ask do I really want this right now? What am I willing to deal with to see this happen?

And this is where scripture tells us that God prepares a table for us in the presence of our enemies. The Lord has set this up as a place for the enemy to taunt you, but you have a choice to sit at the table or keep battling the enemy.

I have been able to watch two people go into the same business at the same time. One had grown up in a business family and his father mentored him. The other did not have a family acquainted with starting or running businesses and he had no mentor. The first time that a dry season happened, the second one decided he needed to go back to working for an employer. The other had the mentality that this happens in business, and he just needs to keep doing what he does.

Many claim this scripture of the Lord setting a table, but they don't choose to sit at the table. They approach the table, but they are still trying to gauge if the table is really for them. But if you choose to, you sit down because you know this is your place. The enemy still shouts those lies and doubts, there is still action to be taken, but you simply live in the knowledge that a place has been prepared for me at this table and I will enjoy what the Lord is giving me more than I worry about what the enemy says.

Where do you receive resistance? It may just be life asking you if you really want this right now. If the answer is yes, then know the lies and the growing pains will be there, but so will the blessing of the Lord.

CHAPTER 10

Accountability and Correction

Those The Father Loves, He Disciplines

Our first 3 keys to really developing as a mature follower of Christ were Joy, Attachment, and Group Identity. We added being able to find our individual identity with a group. All of these things help us become someone who doesn't trip up over the small things nor wavers with every little doctrine that people bring up.

And he gave the apostles, the prophets, the evangelists, the shepherds and teachers, to equip the saints for the work of ministry, for building up the body of Christ, until we all attain to the unity of the faith and of the knowledge of the Son of God, to mature manhood, to the measure of the stature of the fullness of Christ, so that we may no longer be children, tossed to and fro by the waves and carried about by every wind of doctrine, by human cunning, by craftiness in deceitful schemes. Rather, speaking the truth in love, we are to grow up in every way into him who is the head, into Christ, from whom the whole body, joined and held together by every joint with which it is equipped, when each part is working properly, makes the body grow so that it builds itself up in love. Ephesians 4:11-16 (ESV)

The main part of us having leaders who can equip us is for us to cling to Christ as the center and not every little teaching. In this way, we grow and look like Christ. In the beginning of the book, I said you can't solely rely on reading a book for your growth. We all need people around us.

Now, we are going to talk about something many people cringe at, accountability and correction. However, we know that God is love and always does things for our good which should make us feel fine about it, right? But it often doesn't. But being able to maintain joy and having attachment to the person, helps us know that we aren't being held accountable for the sake of us getting into trouble. Instead, it is because they have seen us acting outside of our identity and are calling us back into it. Our identity is where we are full of righteousness, peace, and joy in the Holy Spirit. It is where we maintain the spirit of love, power, and a sound mind that He has given us.

A couple of scriptures to hold onto:

My son, do not despise the LORD's discipline or be weary of his reproof, for the LORD reproves him whom he loves, as a father the son in whom he delights. Proverbs 3:11-12 (ESV) For the Lord disciplines the one he loves, and chastises every son whom he receives. Hebrews 12:6 (ESV)

Again, this draws us back into that we are having the tough conversations because we are family. If a job is getting ready to let you go, they aren't going to have the tough conversations with you. They are going to let you go and let your next boss do that.

Jesus addresses this in **Matthew 18:15-17**. Paul spoke about it in 1 Corinthians.

"If your brother sins against you, go and tell him his fault, between you and him alone. If he listens to you, you have gained your brother. But if he does not listen, take one or two others along with you, that every charge may be established by the evidence of two or three witnesses. If he refuses to listen to them, tell it to the church. And if he refuses to listen

even to the church, let him be to you as a Gentile and a tax collector."

The whole point of taking these steps is to try and protect the person's dignity first and restore them. Taking it before two or three allows mediators to ensure it is done in love and that all sides are seen. Additionally, it also allows them one more step before going before everyone.

The last step is really for when we are letting our narcissism get the best of us. All of us deal with narcissism on some level. But there is a difference between feeling hurt by being confronted and seeing anyone who confronts us as an enemy. For that second group, the only way for them to truly have a chance of staying in the "family" is for everyone to know what is going on. Otherwise, they will do whatever they need to do to make sure at least a few who don't know the conversation are on their side.

The last step is to basically break the relationship with them. Some people have a hard time holding others accountable for their actions. It can feel wrong putting guilt or shame on someone. **But 2 Corinthians 7:10 says, "For godly grief produces a repentance that leads to salvation without regret, whereas worldly grief produces death."**

There are times we need healthy shame to grow because we need the feeling of discomfort to rise above our level to rise high enough before we choose to change. However, there is a difference between toxic shame and healthy shame.

Toxic Shame-Breaks connection, is vague, calls the person bad, and gives no way to correct things.
Healthy Shame-Keeps connection, is specific, addresses the action, and gives opportunity to correct.

For example, let's say a high school football player purposely hits someone late because he is frustrated. It costs the team 15 yards where they would have gained 10.

A toxic coach grabs him by the facemask, tells him he's an idiot and tells him to go sit on the bench. The kid sits embarrassed and feeling like a failure and works himself into more of a funk.

A healthy coach grabs the player and says, "Is that the kind of team we are? Do you understand that your frustrations just cost your team? Go sit down and think about how you're going to make it up to your team."

Again, all of this is to make sure that we maintain family identity. Because when we don't feel joyful, powerful, free, etc. we tend to revert to self-preservation tactics. And knowing that we have an attachment means we can trust them to have this conversation with us. If they didn't want to stay attached, they wouldn't bother having the conversation.

Because we already had the group identity, the traits we learned from the beatitudes and parables, we know what to expect in the conversation rather than feeling like we are being held accountable to something we weren't ready for.

A last thought: When we hold each other accountable to identity, we are saying, "I know what you look like at your best. I'm not seeing that right now. What is going on?"

In this way, I'm holding you to account for your ability. It's the level I've seen you be at. I'm not trying to hold a record of your wrong or holding you to an account for your disability. **Accountability is holding you to an account for your ability not for your disability.** However, if you're not doing what I know you can, or being who I know you can be, what are you filling that time and energy with?

CHAPTER 11

Bear Fruit, Much Fruit, Fruit that Remains

Last time, we started talking about accountability and correction and how to carry it out. But knowing why is a helpful piece. We talked about being able to stay in relationship mode. But for me as the one being held accountable, maybe I'm thinking about myself in the moment, and it is hard for me to think about keeping the relationship. What's in it for me to be held accountable?

Go check out the Parable of the True Vine and the Branches in John 15:1-17

Jesus is the true vine. Our Father is the vine dresser or gardener. And we are the branches. **If we remain connected to Jesus we bear good fruit. Just like Matthew 7:16 says, "You will recognize them by their fruits. Are grapes gathered from thornbushes, or figs from thistles? (ESV)** What you produce is largely based on who you are connected to. (Attachment, Group Identity)

Apart from Him we can do nothing. I believe this has multiple layers to it, one of which is simply that the Lord is the One holding everything together. But another layer is simply that I can do nothing of eternal significance, even as a believer.

> **For no one can lay a foundation other than that which is laid, which is Jesus Christ. Now if anyone builds on the foundation with gold, silver, precious stones, wood, hay, straw— each one's work will become manifest, for the Day will disclose it, because it will be revealed by fire, and the fire will test what sort of work each one has**

**done. If the work that anyone has built on the
foundation survives, he will receive a reward. If
anyone's work is burned up, he will suffer loss, though
he himself will be saved, but only through fire. 1
Corinthians 3:11-15 (ESV)**

Later on, if someone asks if I did anything that is of value, but I
don't actually have anything, it is as though I didn't do anything at
all. **A great quote from minister D.L. Moody, "Our greatest fear
should not be of failure, but of succeeding at something that
doesn't really matter."**

**Those that don't bear fruit are cut off and thrown into the fire.
Those that bear fruit are pruned.** They are pruned so that they
can bear more and better fruit.

Grape vines will continue to grow and grow unless they are pruned.
But when they grow out too far, they stop bearing fruit and what fruit
is produced is not as big or juicy because the branch can't deliver
enough nutrients.

It's the same thing with us. We must allow God to prune us in order
to keep producing good fruit. This isn't just pruning bad stuff out. It's
pruning good stuff out as well. When we do too much our fruit isn't
actually as good.

When we do too much, we are usually squeezing God out from
being part of our daily lives. We go from being Marys to Marthas.
We as the branches aren't getting as many nutrients and those
nutrients aren't getting to where they can produce good fruit. This is
how God keeps us in a good state of growth rather than trying to
become overproducers like our culture likes to promote.

What is God pruning us for?
1. **To bear fruit**
2. **To bear much fruit**
3. **To bear fruit that remains**

This is a great pattern for helping us understand where we are in life.
1. Am I cut off from the Lord? Am I still attached? Well, do I have fruit?
2. If I don't have fruit and am cut off...I'm probably not asking any of these questions.
3. Good fruit can be that my life is turning around. It can be that I'm starting to pray and read my Bible more. It could be that I'm starting to serve people more.
4. Then, if I feel like too much is going on and I'm not seeing the fruit for the amount that I am doing, is God trying to prune me back?

My Story
Some years ago, I was in the business world. I was doing my financial advisory business, but it always felt like a grind. On the side, my wife and I had started up our own ministry and started ministering again.

As I was working one day, I heard God say, "Do you feel like I have cut you off?" I said no. He asked, "How do you know?" I said, "I have too much fruit."

He said, "Then I need to prune you. Where do you see the best fruit? Where do you see the most fruit? Where do you see fruit that lasts? Is it in business or ministry?" For each of these, I had to say ministry. This is just my life; I know plenty of guys who do business well and it is their ministry. But they love doing it, they could do it all day and night if needed and still be happy helping others with their business.

For me it was through ministry. He started the process of moving me out of business. We need to understand, accountability is a

wonderful thing. I want to get to the end and hear, "Well done, My good and faithful servant." I want to have work that passes through the flames. I want to have fruit that remains. The Lord loves staying with us in the process and helping us mature. He is faithful to growing us into a pure and spotless Bride.

CHAPTER 12

Five Fold Ministry and the Effective Church

Five Fold Crash Course

We've been covering topics like finding your place, accountability, and bearing fruit. But what does a healthy church look like? What does a church that you can grow the best in look like? Because without a healthy church, it's hard for everyone to find their place and grow, and it's hard for the Church to be a full expression of Jesus on the earth.

This chapter is going to basically be a crash course in the Five Fold Ministry. The Five Fold Ministry is laid out in **Ephesians 4** and consists of Apostles, Prophets, Teachers, Evangelists, and Pastors.

There are two sets of gifts that it says God gave to His Church. The first is Gifts of the Holy Spirit **1 Corinthians 12:4-11 (NIV)** and these gifts are given by the Holy Spirit to all believers in order for the Church to continue the work of Jesus on the earth.

> **There are different kinds of gifts, but the same Spirit distributes them. There are different kinds of service, but the same Lord. There are different kinds of working, but in all of them and in everyone it is the same God at work.**
>
> **Now to each one the manifestation of the Spirit is given for the common good. To one there is given through the Spirit a message of wisdom, to another a message**

of knowledge by means of the same Spirit, to another faith by the same Spirit, to another gifts of healing by that one Spirit, to another miraculous powers, to another prophecy, to another distinguishing between spirits, to another speaking in different kinds of tongues,[a] and to still another the interpretation of tongues. All these are the work of one and the same Spirit, and he distributes them to each one, just as he determines.

Then there are the Gifts Jesus left the Church **Ephesians 4:11-16**

Christ himself gave the apostles, the prophets, the evangelists, the pastors and teachers, to equip his people for works of service, so that the body of Christ may be built up until we all reach unity in the faith and in the knowledge of the Son of God and become mature, attaining to the whole measure of the fullness of Christ.

Then we will no longer be infants, tossed back and forth by the waves, and blown here and there by every wind of teaching and by the cunning and craftiness of people in their deceitful scheming. Instead, speaking the truth in love, we will grow to become in every respect the mature body of him who is the head, that is, Christ. From him the whole body, joined and held together by every supporting ligament, grows and builds itself up in love, as each part does its work.

Ephesians 2:19, 20 also says, "Consequently, you are no longer foreigners and strangers, but fellow citizens with God's people and also members of his household, built on the foundation of the apostles and prophets, with Christ Jesus himself as the chief cornerstone." (NIV)

Something to note about this scripture is simply that scripture can have many layers to it. Speaking of the apostles and prophets here can be speaking of the fact that Christ is the cornerstone, and the foundation that is laid is Christ's apostles' testimony to Him and the prophets' foretelling of Him.

And it can also be referred to when a church is raised up in a certain location, the message of Jesus is the forefront. And extending from that is an apostle or apostles introducing the culture of heaven (salvation, forgiveness, honor, signs, and wonders, etc.) followed up by prophets giving detail as to how God wants to introduce that into a region (i.e., God wants us to minister to the homeless in the park first, or single moms, etc.)

1 Corinthians 12:27-31 is another important scripture to look at concerning the Five Fold.

> **Now you are the body of Christ, and each one of you is a part of it. And God has placed in the church first of all apostles, second prophets, third teachers, then miracles, then gifts of healing, of helping, of guidance, and of different kinds of tongues. Are all apostles? Are all prophets? Are all teachers? Do all work miracles? Do all have gifts of healing? Do all speak in tongues[a]? Do all interpret? Now eagerly desire the greater gifts. (NIV)**

Again, it's important to look at the context of the scripture. Paul is talking about how these things play out in gatherings. People were trying to one-up each other in the Corinthian church. One person would prophesy and another would feel they needed to as well in order to be seen as equally spiritual. The same with teaching and all the other giftings.

A lot of people would bring up that this means you are either one thing or another, but you can't operate in all of these. This is one place where we are going to look at how to reconcile scriptures that seem like they are saying opposing things.

Ephesians 4 says that the five fold is to train and equip the Body until we come to unity and maturity in the faith, while 1 Corinthians says not all of us walk in everything.

Ephesians is talking about how we walk in general, where 1 Corinthians is addressing how we carry it out in a gathering. In a gathering, not only would it take too much time if all of us thought we needed to fulfill each part to everyone else in the room, but it causes the feeling of competition. But I also can't expect everybody to accept me as everything. There are certain things people will automatically look at me for. Some may be more of a guide, some for comfort, some may be teachers, etc. But most likely, everyone won't see me as everything. Some may like my teaching, but never take comfort or guidance from me because I'm too direct.

However, Ephesians 4 talks about us being raised up into maturity where I look like Christ.

Apostolic = brings the culture of heaven. Governmental, helps put people into the correct places. Plants churches.
- **Their heart naturally asks: "Who needs to know what heaven is like?"**

Prophetic = hearing God in the moment about a relevant situation.
- **Their heart asks: "Who needs to know how to hear God's voice?"**

Teacher = loves to break down the details of what universal teachings scripture says about life and help others know how to process the scriptures
- **Their heart asks: "What do our people need to know about the truths the Bible talks about? How can I design a curriculum that allows people to renew their minds?"**

Pastoral = want to care for the people's needs and take care of the administrative/logistical sides of the church.
- **Their heart asks: "Are my people ok? Who needs help?"**

Evangelistic = wants to tell people about Jesus.
Their heart asks: "Where are people that need to know Jesus?"

When there is a difference between the Gift and the Office (although in Eph. 4 it is talking about the offices as being a gift from Jesus). For example, between being apostolic and being an apostle. Someone filling the office in the church is someone who is able to equip others in that gift. An apostle trains people to be apostolic. If the purpose of the Five Fold is to train the Body to be mature, then they are training each person to be able to flow in each gifting as the moment calls for it.

The biggest example is that we are all called to evangelize and to care for others. Scripture also tells us that we all may prophesy. If we know that we are all called to fulfill pieces of the evangelist, pastor, and prophet, we can deduce that we are also called to fulfill pieces of the apostle and teacher as well.

You should never be in a position to say, "That's not my job," or, "I have to go find someone who can do that." If someone needs to be cared about, you can do any of them. (Bring heaven's culture of righteousness, peace, and joy. Let them know what God is saying. Renew their mind through the scriptures. Tell them about Jesus. Or take care of their needs.)

There are many pieces to the Body. The reason we are looking into this is because each person plays a part. Which one of the five, do you think is naturally you? Many people even lean towards two. If you can't figure out who you are because you feel like you're a little bit of all of them, you may be apostolic.

And in order to make sure things don't get off balance, we need to remember that 1 Corinthians 13 tells us that if we aren't doing things from love, we are a clanging cymbal, a noisy gong, we are nothing.

The Importance of the Five Fold Order

Now let's hammer on why there is the order that is laid out, and why it makes sense. Let's go back to **1 Corinthians 12:27-31.** Why does this make sense to have apostolic, prophetic, and so on? It isn't so that there is a hierarchy. That is the kind of thinking that creates one of two systems, one where everyone tries to reach the top and another that disregards God-given order because they are afraid it allows for egos. The Five Fold are more of a checks and balance system in the way they play out. But it still makes sense to start with the apostles, prophets, and so on.

Typically, modern churches start with pastors and teachers. When this is the case, it isn't requiring most people to grow. They are focused on being cared for and learning head knowledge. A lot of this is based on shaping a teacher to look like teachers in our education system where you merely learn to regurgitate. These systems end up with people not wanting to move as much because they always feel like they aren't whole enough or don't know enough.

Another reason this happens is because many don't understand that the positions of these offices are really to train people to move as one, not just to take care of people and give them head knowledge.

An apostle is telling you to shift culture, prophets are training you to hear God, and evangelists are training you to get people. These offices are much more experiential and movement focused.

You can pastor, teach, and even evangelize from a completely earthly point of view. When this happens, pastors just coddle people, teachers turn scripture into self-help or legalism, and evangelists just tell people to receive Jesus or burn. But the roles of apostle and prophet demand that they are looking at heaven and hearing God.

This causes the role of pastor to function under the premise of keeping healthy function and correcting real issues that arise. Too many times, pastors are dealing with people who aren't active enough, so they have a new complaint every week. And it causes the teacher to teach according to experience rather than theory that can be more highly debated. It also means the teachings will stick that much more.

A church that functions like the Bible is mentioning actually looks like this:

Apostles are culture setters, showing people the culture of heaven. (Salvation, forgiveness, miracles, signs, wonders, healing, etc.) This brings people into an awareness of the difference between the culture of our Father and the culture of the world.

It also can bring in the specific culture of a church body. They may be more focused toward being missional and pastoring their neighborhood or a heavy emphasis on evangelism. It could also be that they are a church to take members of the Body in the area deeper, train them more, or even to set up ministries like prayer houses. Apostles are typically church and ministry starters.

When the culture is set, prophets can give more accuracy into carrying out the mission.

Then teachers can train people on the Biblical foundations of carrying out the mission.

Evangelists take people out to carry out the mission.

Pastors take care of members of the Body who are dealing with life issues or who have been hurt by them so they can get back to being part of the mission.

When that isn't happening, the church isn't missional, there are a lot of questions of "why" that need to be answered. Why evangelize? To get people into seats? Why pastor? To make people feel better?

But when a church is missional like this, from apostle through to pastor you see:

Why apostle you? Because God has a mission and purpose for this area to bring heaven to earth.

Why be a prophetic voice and train people in it? Because we need to hear God's specifics on how He wants to carry out His mission in our city.

Why teach you? Because you need to know that this is a God idea rather than just some man's. We want to know the scriptural truths and details about carrying out the mission and know that it has the backing of the Church for centuries and generations.

Why evangelize to you? Because God has a plan for this city, and He wants to include everyone in it. You have a future with this city, and we want to pull you in on the mission.

Why pastor you? Because you have a part in what God is doing. Without you, your giftings, and your heart, it isn't the same. We want to help you through life issues, so you are free and powerful.

This starts to make sense as a functional body of people. We are no longer just doing activities to do them. They have a purpose. We aren't a group of people where a small percentage are taking care of everyone else, but a whole body of movers. We aren't just waiting to be more taken care of or to learn more. We are doing something, so we learn and take care of each other so that we can continue moving forward in manifesting God's Kingdom into our city.

At the beginning of this chapter, we shared that this is all about us learning to love like our Father and carrying out His purposes together. And everybody plays a part. What parts do you see yourself leaning toward?

CHAPTER 13

The Spiritual Disciplines

The Disciplines of Abstinence

The spiritual disciplines can seem like a boring topic. To some, they may even call it pointless. They may say, "Those were things we needed to do under the Old Covenant, but we don't need to do them now that Jesus has done it all.

These people don't understand that God gave us these things not as acts that accomplish the things that we are looking for. These disciplines allow us to take part in our growth. **"So neither the one who plants nor the one who waters is anything, but only God, who makes things grow." 1 Corinthians 3:7 (NIV)** They don't twist God's arm, but they position us to receive what He is already giving to us.

These are not righteous acts, meaning that they are not things that we are commanded to do. Rather they are ways that we can practically be involved with our own spiritual growth. If we notice we are lacking in certain things, or we need to grow in certain areas, there are disciplines that we can look at to specifically help us out.

Even Jesus did the disciplines. Again, they have a benefit of keeping us in check so that we can hear the Father.

Do you not know that in a race all the runners run, but only one receives the prize? So run that you may obtain it. Every athlete exercises self-control in all things. They do it to receive a perishable wreath, but we are imperishable. So, I do not run aimlessly; I do not box as one beating the air. But I discipline

my body and keep it under control, lest after preaching to others I myself should be disqualified. 1 Corinthians 9:24-27 (ESV)

The problem with the disciplines is that they will build up whatever mindset you are doing them in. The Pharisees fasted and it built up their self-righteousness. Many can look at these thinking it is just for those with spiritual pride. But that's why the purpose can never be about simply doing the discipline, nor for showing others.

The question is always what am I doing this unto? It's not simply about what I am giving up. Either I'm doing this to put my flesh in check, or to come more in line with what God is doing, or to position myself to hear God better. Etc.

As we dive in, we are going to divide the disciplines up into two categories:
Disciplines of Abstinence and Disciplines of Engagement

The Disciplines of Abstinence are intended to keep us small. We sometimes have a tendency to take on way too much, or we let our life get filled with clutter.

It is a lot like a house getting too much stuff in it. It may be all the best looking, expensive stuff. But if there is too much, it still just looks like a mess and becomes a hassle to take care of.

During the practice of these disciplines, you will often feel frustrated. "UGH! The things I like to do I can't do! What do I fill my time with?! I deserve to be able to say something, have my money, eat!!!" The things that have helped your brain produce the right chemicals to help you feel normal and happy are taken away and it reveals who you really are.

You're not grumpy because you haven't eaten. You're grumpy because you're a grumpy person. It's just that usually the food you eat helps your body create the energy and endorphins that help you feel normal. But now you're seeing who you really are.

Solitude
Yet the news about him spread all the more, so that crowds of people came to hear him and to be healed of their sicknesses. But Jesus often withdrew to lonely places and prayed. Luke 5:15-16 (NIV)

We can get used to our value being from hanging around people that if we were to be by ourselves, we would feel worthless. We have to know that God and I have the same relationship around people and being alone.

Likewise, getting alone helps me decide who I really am. What is my true personality? Who did God make me to be?

We can get so used to even getting online and seeing how people are, and then modeling ourselves off of someone else. This means solitude really should even mean a putting away of social media and t.v. in order to look at who God made me to be.

Silence
We could couple this with solitude, except that you can also take times to practice this while around others.

He was oppressed and afflicted, yet he did not open his mouth; he was led like a lamb to the slaughter, and as a sheep before its shearers is silent, so he did not open his mouth. Isaiah 53:7 (NIV)

We often feel a need to defend ourselves. Or we feel our words can make us seem more valuable. But we are never more or less valuable to God. But like the scripture above said, we practice self-control like an athlete. Therefore, we should even do this with our tongues.

Not many of you should become teachers, my fellow believers, because you know that we who teach will be judged more strictly. We all stumble in many ways. Anyone who is never at fault in what they say is perfect, able to keep their whole body in check.

When we put bits into the mouths of horses to make them obey us, we can turn the whole animal. Or take ships as an example. Although they are so large and are driven by strong winds, they are steered by a very small rudder wherever the pilot wants to go. Likewise, the tongue is a small part of the body, but it makes great boasts. Consider what a great forest is set on fire by a small spark. The tongue also is a fire, a world of evil among the parts of the body. It corrupts the whole body, sets the whole course of one's life on fire, and is itself set on fire by hell.

All kinds of animals, birds, reptiles, and sea creatures are being tamed and have been tamed by mankind, but no human being can tame the tongue. It is a restless evil, full of deadly poison.

With the tongue we praise our Lord and Father, and with it we curse human beings, who have been made in God's likeness. Out of the same mouth come praise and cursing. My brothers and sisters, this should not be. Can both fresh water and saltwater flow from the same spring? My brothers and sisters, can a fig tree bear olives, or a grapevine bear figs? Neither can a salt spring produce fresh water. James 3:1-12 (NIV)

Fasting

There are many benefits to fasting. This is just a quick take on it; however, there are many good books that cover it in greater depth.

Even Jesus fasted for forty days in the wilderness. The issue here is that it is something we need for life. Even our legitimate needs and rights need to be put on the table in order for us to become less selfish. Fasting is one of the easiest ways to reveal our selfishness. But what are we fasting unto? I don't simply want to not eat to not eat. But that time and energy can be placed somewhere else for a time.

There are also many practical purposes of fasting. It is not wrong to want to do it to lose some weight and be healthier. God wants us to have healthy bodies. As we age, and our bodies take on stress, they start to form mutated cells. After 72 hours of nothing but water, your body starts to eat those imperfect cells. In more ways than one, this is a way God has given us to clean up our bodies.

It also takes away the endorphins that are usually created to help us stay in a good mood. That means it reveals a lot about places we are selfish, impatient, etc.

Isaiah chapter 58 gives us a great picture of yes, we fast from something, but it is much more about what we are fasting unto that matters.

When the disciples returned to Jesus speaking with the woman at the well, they thought he must be hungry. But he replied, "But he said to them, "I have food to eat that you know nothing about." John 4:32

Then John's disciples came and asked him, "How is it that we and the Pharisees fast often, but your disciples do not fast?" Jesus answered, "How can the guests of the bridegroom mourn while he is with them? The time will come when the bridegroom will be taken from them; then they will fast. Matthew 9:14-15

In the book of Acts, the apostles fasted while appointing another apostle to take Judas' place and when appointing Paul and Barnabas. It is a way of putting our hearts and minds into a place where the decision we are making or endeavor we are on right now is more important than any other thing we have going on.

The early Church had a practice of fasting twice a week. They would give the food or the money for it to the poor.

What is the point of fasting? It is a great way to starve our flesh and practice self-discipline, especially while using prayer to build our spirit. I liken it to when I used to fight. Many times, I would go to the gym and workout first to make myself tired before going to fight training. Now when I would train, I wouldn't be able to use my speed and explosiveness. Now I would need to rely on my technique. Fasting is very similar.

One thing I have found fasting to be very useful for is fasting toward freedom from addiction or to press in for more breakthrough in seeing more things like healings or deliverance happen, or to know an aspect of the Lord better.

Jesus said that after He left His disciples would fast. Why would that be? Well, of course you want to party while the Bridegroom is there. But also, because you could simply ask Him things about Himself, or directions, or for consolation or comfort. But many times, now that He is gone, we have a hard time hearing the Lord for direction. Fasting is a great way to clear the lines and be zeroed in on hearing the Lord better.

Frugality
Again, some of this comes down to us seeing what the world uses its money for. It teaches us what is important, what is luxuries or even wasteful, and how to prioritize. Many in our culture today suffer financially for little else than they have trouble not wanting too many options.

Why spend money on what is not bread, and your labor on what does not satisfy? Listen, listen to me, and eat what is good, and you will delight in the richest of fare. Isaiah 55:2

Chastity
This one is rather simple if we only think about it in regard to sex. But on a bigger scale, intimacy is really us being able to find deeper connection with another being. It is knowing someone and being fully known without any guilt or shame. This is about us finding our intimacy in God.

Again, if we think about this in terms of sex, it makes some things clear. One of the bigger issues of today is people falling into lust and having premarital sex. They often think this creates a deeper sense of intimacy. But that isn't necessarily true, but it can cause unhealthy attachment. Even in marriage, for someone to only want sex but not to know, serve, and honor their spouse will result in relational strain because there is no depth.

This transfers into other relationships as well. It can be easy to think that if you simply give someone a gift or some nice words that it will cause the person to feel attached to you. It may for some. The point is that over time, you do need to truly get to know that person and their love language. The point is not to just do the cheap stuff that comes easy to you but to do the deep stuff that truly ministers to them.

Secrecy
This could be tied to silence as well. However, it is bigger than that. We have a culture that loves to thrive on knowledge.

So, they hurried off and found Mary and Joseph, and the baby, who was lying in the manger. When they had seen him, they spread the word concerning what had been told them about this child, and all who heard it were amazed at what the

shepherds said to them. But Mary treasured up all these things and pondered them in her heart. Luke 2:16-19 (NIV)

A lot of the time what we do with knowledge, is that we automatically want to release it. We don't realize the benefits of letting it build and go deeper in our hearts. Often people want to "stand around the water cooler" and say what they know about stuff. Most of what we see on the news anymore has little value than to release it as a form of gossip and make us feel good for saying that we know something. People only used to care about news they could do something about.

Even with personal goals, people like to tell everyone what they are doing. But then they get the dopamine release in their brain, and it tells them it feels just as good as if they actually did the thing. Therefore, they don't accomplish their goals.

God doesn't value you any more just because you have something to say. On the other hand, there is a great value, a deepening of revelation and conviction, that comes when we refuse to prematurely release what we have.

Sacrifice
What is real sacrifice? It isn't really when we are giving up things that don't matter to us. It is when we are giving to the point that it makes us feel it. It's the things that we have a right to. The things that are necessary.

Again, none of these things are "righteous acts". As is stated in 1 Samuel 15:22, "To obey is better than sacrifice."

Did Jesus need to go to the cross? No. But for our sake, He gave up His life.

Practical Use of the Disciplines of Abstinence
Now the practical place to run with these is to make a regular practice of them. And then also to know how to read your life

trends. If you find you are having a hard time connecting with the Lord, or you find yourself looking for self-worth from somewhere else, these give you a practical activity that will help you empty out the distractions in your life.

The Disciplines of Engagement

Just as the Disciplines of Abstinence help us clean out our proverbial house, the Discipline of Engagement help us put the right and most important things in first. Again, these aren't "righteous acts". But they are beneficial.

In Matthew 6:16-18 Jesus said, "When you fast, do not look somber as the hypocrites do, for they disfigure their faces to show others they are fasting. Truly I tell you, they have received their reward in full. But when you fast, put oil on your head and wash your face, so that it will not be obvious to others that you are fasting, but only to your Father, who is unseen; and your Father, who sees what is done in secret, will reward you.

And for prayer, which we will cover today, He says, **"And when you pray, do not be like the hypocrites, for they love to pray standing in the synagogues and on the street corners to be seen by others. Truly I tell you, they have received their reward in full. But when you pray, go into your room, close the door and pray to your Father, who is unseen. Then your Father, who sees what is done in secret, will reward you." Matthew 6:5-6 (NIV)**

As we said last time, the question for all of these is what are we doing it unto. These scriptures are pointing out that we do it for an eternal reward from our Father, not for man's approval. We want to do these things in secret because if we don't let them sink into us, but instead do it for men to recognize, then we will value that and miss our eternal reward, which is really a closer, more mature relationship with the Lord. It matches up with our discipline of secrecy.

This isn't saying that if you happened to simply mention it to anyone that you have totally given up your reward. It's simply saying, doing the act out of spiritual pride will strip your reward.

The Disciplines of Abstinence were about keeping us small. The Disciplines of Engagement are more about adding to us what God wants to add to us.

The Discipline of Study
2 Timothy 3:16-17 All Scripture is God-breathed and is useful for teaching, rebuking, correcting and training in righteousness, so that the servant of God may be thoroughly equipped for every good work. (NIV)

Hebrews 4:12 For the word of God is alive and active. Sharper than any double-edged sword, it penetrates even to dividing soul and spirit, joints and marrow; it judges the thoughts and attitudes of the heart. (NIV)

I want to give a fuller version of what studying is though. All things must be backed up by scripture in order to be considered truth. Like Paul and the Bereans where they searched the scriptures daily to see if what he was saying was true. But there are other places to study.

For since the creation of the world God's invisible qualities— his eternal power and divine nature—have been clearly seen, being understood from what has been made, so that people are without excuse. Romans 1:20

The question would be, "How do Christians who don't have the scriptures study? How did Abraham, Isaac, and Jacob?" They studied what they saw, but everything they gained had to be verified with what they knew to be true of the Lord. In this way, you can constantly see God everywhere and study everywhere. It's also important because then you are seeing if what you are pulling from scripture is actually true in life or if you need to tweak it a little bit.

Proverbs 4:5-7 Get wisdom, get understanding; do not forget my words or turn away from them. Do not forsake wisdom, and she will protect you; love her, and she will watch over you. The beginning of wisdom is this: Get wisdom. Though it cost all you have, get understanding.

Worship

The first four commandments given to Moses. **"You shall have no other gods before me. "You shall not make for yourself an image in the form of anything in heaven above or on the earth beneath or in the waters below. You shall not bow down to them or worship them; for I, the Lord your God, am a jealous God, punishing the children for the sin of the parents to the third and fourth generation of those who hate me, but showing love to a thousand generations of those who love me and keep my commandments. You shall not misuse the name of the Lord your God, for the Lord will not hold anyone guiltless who misuses his name. Remember the Sabbath day, to keep it holy." - Exodus 20:3-8 (NIV)**

To the extent you hold the Lord as Holy and good, you will treat things from Him as such. We were made to be creatures of worship. And we can't hide what we worship because we become like what we worship. This is why God tells us to worship Him only.
Even in the Gospels when asked what the greatest commandment is, Jesus quotes Moses as, "Love the Lord with all your heart, with all your soul, with all your mind, and with all your strength."

So what is worship? It isn't just music. Worship should be something we do with every part of our life. The Hebrews didn't separate being in the synagogue from the rest of life.

Therefore, I urge you, brothers and sisters, in view of God's mercy, to offer your bodies as a living sacrifice, holy and

pleasing to God—this is your true and proper worship. Do not conform to the pattern of this world but be transformed by the renewing of your mind. Then you will be able to test and approve what God's will is—his good, pleasing, and perfect will. Romans 12:1-2

Likewise, Paul tells us here that our worship is to be living sacrifices. And as we let it renew our mind in order that we don't look like the world but we are able to test and approve that God's will is good.

Celebration

In the Old Testament, God gave the Israelites specific times and ways to celebrate. Those things became reminders of what God had done. Although it says that God rested on the seventh day of the creation story, we take it to mean He did nothing. Resting can be part of celebrating. And what it actually says is that He rested from His work. Celebration is important for us to have regular remembrances of what God has done.

Service

"You are the light of the world. A town built on a hill cannot be hidden. Neither do people light a lamp and put it under a bowl. Instead, they put it on its stand, and it gives light to everyone in the house. 16In the same way, let your light shine before others, that they may see your good deeds and glorify your Father in heaven. Matthew 5:14-16 So our serving actually causes others to praise God.

Dear friends, let us love one another, for love comes from God. Everyone who loves has been born of God and knows God.God is love. Whoever lives in love lives in God, and God in them. Whoever claims to love God yet hates a brother or sister is a liar. For whoever does not love their brother and

sister, whom they have seen, cannot love God, whom they have not seen. 1 John 4:7, 16, 20

Many times, Jesus says that to love Him means to obey His commands. And multiple times, like **John 15:12 "My command is this: Love each other as I have loved you."** That means there is a direct link between loving others and loving God. Love looks like something. You can't just say you love people. It is shown by what you do and say.

Colossians 3:23-24 Whatever you do, work at it with all your heart, as working for the Lord, not for human masters, since you know that you will receive an inheritance from the Lord as a reward. It is the Lord Christ you are serving.

"Salt is good, but if it loses its saltiness, how can it be made salty again? It is fit neither for the soil nor for the manure pile; it is thrown out." Luke 14:34-35

The salt they were talking about was used for fertilizer and sanitizer. It took a lot in order to fertilize a field or to sanitize the soil in their backyard that was used for an outhouse. Our good deeds, our saltiness, is used by God to grow what is of the Kingdom and sterilize what is not.

Prayer
This is really having a conversation with God, not merely racking off our list of needs and wants. It is us coming into a meeting with the Creator of the universe who knows everything and can fix everything. My goal should be to come out different than I went in. It should cause me to reflect the fruit of the Spirit and show the power of God.

Therefore, confess your sins to each other and pray for each other so that you may be healed. The prayer of a righteous person is powerful and effective. James 5:16 (NIV)

Matthew 6:5-8 Jesus says, "And when you pray, do not be like the hypocrites, for they love to pray standing in the synagogues and on the street corners to be seen by others. Truly I tell you, they have received their reward in full. But when you pray, go into your room, close the door and pray to your Father, who is unseen. Then your Father, who sees what is done in secret, will reward you. And when you pray, do not keep on babbling like pagans, for they think they will be heard because of their many words. Do not be like them, for your Father knows what you need before you ask him."

The Lord's Prayer which follows in **Matthew 6:9-13** gives us a pattern to be able to follow. We want to take times, periodically, to not just rush through this, but to actually dwell on those specific points. God is Holy, Heaven is His Kingdom and it's wonderful, we want that Kingdom to come to earth, etc.

Fellowship
They devoted themselves to the apostles' teaching and to fellowship, to the breaking of bread and to prayer. Everyone was filled with awe at the many wonders and signs performed by the apostles. All the believers were together and had everything in common. They sold property and possessions to give to anyone who had need. Every day they continued to meet together in the temple courts. They broke bread in their homes and ate together with glad and sincere hearts, praising God and enjoying the favor of all the people. And the Lord added to their number daily those who were being saved. Acts 2:42-47 (NIV)

And let us consider how we may spur one another on toward love and good deeds, not giving up meeting together, as some are in the habit of doing, but encouraging one another—and all the more as you see the Day approaching. Hebrews 10:24-25 (NIV)

There are multiple reasons for gathering. Teaching is one of them, but it seems to be the main focus in the Western Church. However, that teaching should lead to us having fellowship together as the Family of Christ. And it should be something that encourages us all.

Confession
Therefore, confess your sins to each other and pray for each other so that you may be healed. The prayer of a righteous person is powerful and effective. James 5:16

That confession is not just to talk about obvious sins. Sin is anything that is not of God. We need to confess to one another the places that we are not living up to what we know God's will is in our lives. It does a couple of things. One is that it holds us accountable and keeps us from waiting until things get too far. But it also helps us in that many times we carry condemnation that really isn't for us to carry. Like you may feed into the lie that, "I'm not a good son." There may be things you can do better, but that isn't your identity.

> **"Therefore, if you are offering your gift at the altar and there remember that your brother or sister has something against you, leave your gift there in front of the altar. First go and be reconciled to them; then come and offer your gift.**
>
> **"Settle matters quickly with your adversary who is taking you to court. Do it while you are still together on the way, or your adversary may hand you over to the judge, and the judge may hand you over to the officer, and you may be thrown into prison. Truly I tell you, you will not get out until you have paid the last penny." Matthew 5:23-26**

This is just outright practical. You want to make sure you are taking care of issues as soon as possible. First, to bring peace back into your life sooner. Also, so that it doesn't have to get heated any further.

Other scripture says to settle matters before the sun goes down. When anger is allowed to remain, then you go to sleep, it goes into your subconscious mind. There it is allowed to enter your dreams and cause emotions to be fed.

If it is possible, as far as it depends on you, live at peace with everyone.
Romans 12:18

Submission
Submit yourselves, then, to God. Resist the devil, and he will flee from you. James 4:7

Have confidence in your leaders and submit to their authority, because they keep watch over you as those who must give an account. Do this so that their work will be a joy, not a burden, for that would be of no benefit to you. Hebrews 13:17

> When Jesus had entered Capernaum, a centurion came to him, asking for help. "Lord," he said, "my servant lies at home paralyzed, suffering terribly."
>
> Jesus said to him, "Shall I come and heal him?"
>
> The centurion replied, "Lord, I do not deserve to have you come under my roof. But just say the word, and my servant will be healed. For I myself am a man under authority, with soldiers under me. I tell this one, 'Go,' and he goes; and that one, 'Come,' and he comes. I say to my servant, 'Do this,' and he does it."
>
> When Jesus heard this, he was amazed and said to those following him, "Truly I tell you, I have not found anyone in Israel with such great faith. I say to you that many will come from the east and the west, and will take their places at the feast with Abraham, Isaac and Jacob in the kingdom of heaven. But the subjects of the kingdom will be thrown outside, into the darkness, where there will be weeping and gnashing of teeth."
>
> Then Jesus said to the centurion, "Go! Let it be done just as you believed it would." And his servant was healed at that moment. Matthew 8:5-13

Being able to submit to earthly authority shows you submit to God's authority and have faith in His authority.

Obviously, a lot of what we have talked about has to do with submitting to authority. "**Submit to one another out of reverence for Christ." Ephesians 5:21** This means that submitting to one another is a way that we stay focused on Christ and not simply our own agenda.

Conclusion on the Disciplines

There are people who hang too heavily on one side or the other about the disciplines. Some can make them the focus rather than Jesus. Others can think that they are unimportant and of little use. Some of the disciplines are easily seen as a daily practice such as studying the scripture and prayer while others tend to be used less frequently, like fasting. However, it is important to remember that each of these serve specific purposes. And the main purposes for all of them are to clear out our proverbial house and add in the main things first so that we stay focused on Jesus. My suggestion is to make a regular habit of using both the Disciplines of Abstinence and the Disciplines of Engagement.

CHAPTER 14

The Longings of the Human Heart

The Disciplines help us navigate life. Equally as important is the understanding of what our heart is searching for. We can know how to grow close to the Lord, but without asking what our hearts were designed for, we may sometimes still have confusion about why we are buying into certain lies of the enemy or struggling with certain emotions. We were made with certain longings or desires because we were made in the image of God.

We were made in the image of an incredible God that goes beyond our understanding. And we were designed to live in a state of being exhilarated in God.

I will declare it (Your name), that the love with which You loved Me may be in them. (Jn. 17:26)

God reveals Himself to our spirit and it awakens love in us. We can't love Him without Him giving us the grace and power to love Him. Jesus said that no man could come to Him unless the Father drew him. The very fact that someone wants God is God's gift to us and an expression of His desire for us.

God created the human spirit with seven longings that draw us to Him and reflect His glory in us. These longings reflect who God is and having them allows us to walk with Him. Certain ones can be hard to deal with in our ideas of religion. For example, the longing to be great can feel like we are not being humble, and we should therefore repent of it. However, these have been designed in us and will always be a part of us.

We can't repent or rebuke these away. The only thing we can really do is to pursue them in the way the scriptures and the Holy Spirit direct us to. Each of these longings has a counterfeit. To seek them outside of God's will only leads to shame and regret. The only way to carry them out free from that is to seek them inside of a relationship with Jesus.

One thing we need to understand about these is that God has created us with an incredible appetite for pleasure. But much of the time, we will take what is quicker and easier and forego the greater pleasures He has designed us for. As we seek to answer these longings in our relationship with Jesus, we will experience the "superior pleasures" of the gospel. In this way, we can walk free from a life of the "inferior pleasures" of sin. The result is that we are empowered to love Jesus more. The essence of temptation is to seek to satisfy these longings outside of God's will.

Jesus told the parable of the wheat and the weeds. He said that both are allowed to grow together until the harvest. As we grow closer to Jesus' return, many will walk in unprecedented measures of perversion and woundedness. There will be a great increase of murder, pornography, and the occult. And not only will people follow these lesser, sinful ways of life, Revelation 9:21 says they will defend them. **They did not repent of their murders or sorceries or sexual immorality or thefts. (Rev. 9:21)**

The wheat In that parable stands for those who follow Jesus. Jesus will return for a mature, equally yoked Bride **(Ephesians 5:27)**. In the face of escalating sin, God will bring His people to victory. Only satisfied people who are happy in God will be equipped to stand in that hour. Just as we discussed concerning the Beatitudes, for those who are attached, God will use everything to draw us into deeper relationship and greater character.

LONGING #1: TO KNOW YOU ARE ENJOYED BY GOD
As the Father loved Me, I also have loved you. (Jn. 15:9)

We were all created with a deep craving to be pursued, delighted in, and enjoyed by God, family, and friends. One of the biggest fears people have is the fear of being rejected and the trauma that comes from shame. Feeling like we could have possibly reached a place where God could no longer enjoy us can wreak havoc on our hearts and minds.

When we understand the finished work of the cross, what Jesus did, and why He did it, that longing to be enjoyed by God is fulfilled. God revealing His affections for us releases us to respond with those same emotions.

It can be hard for us to believe that God loves us in our immature stages because we notice our inability to walk everything out yet, but this is a beautiful place because we can't be upset by seeing that unless we want to walk closer to the Lord. There is a difference between rebellion and spiritual immaturity in those who sincerely seek to obey God. God is angry about rebellion but feels affection for immature believers who love Him. God enjoys us even now, in our spiritual immaturity! Jesus described the Father and the angels rejoicing, or feeling joy, over repentant prodigals

Even when Jesus corrects us, He does not reject us. He corrects us because He so desires us. **For whom the LORD loves He corrects, just as a father the son in whom he delights. (Prov. 3:12)**

LONGING #2: THE LONGING TO BE FASCINATED
Your eyes will see the King in His beauty... (Isa. 33:17)

In our spirit, we have a craving to be fascinated. The entertainment industry has figured this out. It's why we love things like roller coasters and movies with more and more CGI. When God reveals Himself to the human spirit we experience "divine entertainment" at its highest.

Like David leading a nation, we do our best when we are living in and being led by a state of constant fascination with God. Without it we get bored and live aimlessly. Being spiritually bored leaves us weak and vulnerable to Satan. But being fascinated by the Lord helps us be strong and equipped to face temptation.

LONGING #3: THE LONGING TO BE DESIRABLE
Let the beauty of the LORD our God be upon us... (Ps. 90:17)

God has created us in a way that when we look at Him, we naturally respond with a desire to also possess and feel His beauty imparted to us. The beauty that God possesses is the very beauty that He imparts to us through His salvation. His own beauty is transferable to humans through Jesus!

To give them beauty for ashes, the oil of joy for mourning. (Isa. 61:3)

It is very common to be obsessed with physical beauty and seek to answer this legitimate longing in a wrong way. Many pursue beauty at great lengths because they feel unsettled without it. But we were meant to pursue beauty from it exuding from Christ within us. This is why **1 Peter 3:3-4 says, "Your beauty should not come from outward adornment, such as elaborate hairstyles and the wearing of gold jewelry or fine clothes. Rather, it should be that of your inner self, the unfading beauty of a gentle and quiet spirit, which is of great worth in God's sight."**

LONGING #4: THE LONGING TO BE GREAT
Whoever desires to become great among you, let him be your servant.

And whoever desires to be first among you, let him be your slave. (Mt. 20:26-27)

God is great and in His image, He created us to be great. This causes us a desire for greatness and success. God created us to be crowned with glory, honor, and nobility. Some misunderstand this and repent of it, hoping to remove it. We can't remove it. We can only repent of trying to pursue it in an illegitimate way. **Whoever does and teaches them [God's commands], he shall be called great in the kingdom of heaven. (Matthew 5:19)**

God meets our longing for greatness by giving us a position of authority with Him. He has seated us in heavenly places with Jesus. **To him who overcomes I will grant to sit with Me on My throne … (Revelation 3:21)**

LONGING #5: WE LONG FOR INTIMACY WITHOUT SHAME
For now, we see in a mirror, dimly, but then face to face. Now I know in part, but then I shall know just as I also am known. (1 Corinthians 13:12)

Intimacy is really to know someone and be fully known without any guilt or shame. It's why we love hearing stories of a husband and wife who stuck it out their entire lives through thick and thin. We want to know that someone wants to really know us, won't use us for the good parts, and won't run from us for the bad parts.

We can trust God because He knows the innermost secrets of our hearts, yet He sent Jesus because He wanted us to come back into a full relationship with Him. To be fully known without shame and to be free from the fear of being left alone is exhilarating. He rejoices and celebrates with us as He shares our triumphs. He understands the secret aspects of our life that are unknown, unnoticed, and misunderstood by others.

Rejoice with those who rejoice…weep with those who weep… (Rom. 12:15)

We can trust that God knows the struggles we go through in life and our fight to stay free from sin. He knows the pain we feel when we have done wrong and feels that with us. He knows what it costs us to press into deeper life with Him, and He celebrates alongside us.

LONGING #6: THE LONGING TO BE WHOLEHEARTED AND
PASSIONATE
**You shall love the LORD your God with all your heart...
(Matthew 22:37)**

We have a deep desire to give our entire selves to something. It's
why we love seeing athletic champions, inspiring artists, and
leaders in different fields of education, industry, medicine, etc. We
know that they have given up many other opportunities, hobbies,
and pleasures to give it all to their passion.

But there are people who have done the same, and sacrificed so
much, to chase pursuits that were not God-given to them. The only
way this can be truly met in us is by doing it as a means to pursue
the heart of Jesus.

The human heart does not work properly in half-heartedness. When
we are passive, we get bored, and when we get bored, we more
easily cave to lusts. In order to be emotionally whole, we must live
wholeheartedly. Walking in wholehearted love for Jesus frees us
from the burnout of spiritual boredom. This is why it is important for
us to keep the Greatest Commandment as first place in our hearts.
It's why we must seek the Kingdom first and let everything else be
added.

LONGING #7: THE LONGING FOR SIGNIFICANCE: TO MAKE A
LASTING IMPACT
**For God is not unjust to forget your work and labor of love
which you have shown toward His name, in that you have
ministered to the saints, and do minister. (Hebrews 6:10)**

We also don't truly live to our fullest when we are only living for
ourselves. The people we marvel about are the people who have
changed the world not only for themselves or even their generation,
but for many after that. There is a saying that the world may never
see something as wonderful as older men who plant trees the
shade of which they know they will never have the pleasure to sit
under.

We tend to think that filling this desire in us, to have long-lasting impact, can only come through doing actions that affect many. But most of the time, the way this happens is through small, seemingly simple acts. Jesus told us in **Matthew 10:42** that if we even gave a cup of cold water in His name it would leave such an impact on His heart that we would never lose our reward.

Well done, good and faithful servant; you were faithful over a few things, I will make you ruler over many things. Enter into the joy of your lord. (Matthew 25:21)

Whatever you do, do it heartily, as to the Lord...knowing that from the Lord you will receive the reward of the inheritance... (Colossians 3:22-25)

Let me say it one last time, these are God-given desires. You will not get them to go away, but if you are not careful, you will pursue them in the wrong way, outside of a relationship with Jesus. The only way to pursue these desires without regret and shame is to see that we only have them because we are made in the image of God and to pursue Him and look like Him by pursuing these desires His way.

CHAPTER 15

Our Everyday Lives

Dealing with the Ups and Downs

We've been discussing understanding natural ways our hearts are made to work and methods to help steer it. But either you've already noticed or it's only a matter of time before you do that bad days are bound to happen.

The methods and understanding we discussed are meant to be our standard operating procedures. They help us in the regular points of life. But there are circumstances in life that can't be helped, including just times that we can't shake the feelings or thoughts we are having.

"Do you now believe?" Jesus replied. "A time is coming and in fact has come when you will be scattered, each to your own home. You will leave me all alone. Yet I am not alone, for my Father is with me.

"I have told you these things, so that in me you may have peace. In this world you will have trouble. But take heart! I have overcome the world." John 16:31-33 (NIV)

Now there were some present at that time who told Jesus about the Galileans whose blood Pilate had mixed with their sacrifices. Jesus answered, "Do you think that these Galileans were worse sinners than all the other Galileans because they suffered this way? I tell you, no! But unless you repent, you too will all perish. Or those eighteen who died when the tower in Siloam fell on them—do you think they were more guilty

than all the others living in Jerusalem? I tell you, no! But unless you repent, you too will all perish." Luke 13:1-5 (NIV)

Jesus told his disciples more than once that troubles can come to you even when you are following Jesus. Jesus knew this was going to be important for His followers. Look how many times we base whether we are following the Lord or not based on if circumstances seem against us.

Some people think if everything is going well, it must be because "you just must really be close with the Lord." And on the other end of the spectrum, we have sayings like, "Higher levels, higher devils." This is especially true in our social media era where we make judgments on someone's life because of what we see on social media even though we have no connection to that person or idea of what is going on with them.

Jesus also said this to help us fight against the Enemy. The only weapon the Enemy has ever had is to lie to us. So, when bad situations in life happen, the Enemy likes to say, "I did that." He wants you to buy into it and think he has more power than he has.

Isaiah 58:8 tells us that our righteousness leads us forward and the glory of the Lord will protect us from behind. God reveals His character through us, and as we follow through with that, the goodness of God that we manifest into the world protects us. (I.e., people whom you've helped will protect your reputation. Those you've helped financially may return the favor. Etc.)

A lot of the attacks on your life should be thwarted by the fruit you've manifested. Guaranteed there will be more attacks because more people will know you, but also there will be more protection.

However, almost any time you start to move in an upward projection in an area of life, you are bound to have something come against you. (I.e., negativity from those thinking you've changed, critics of how you're doing it, lack of finances, being told you don't have enough experience, etc.)

This is just a way life has been set up to ask you if you really want what you are going after. The Lord has set it up that if the Enemy is going to attack you, this is the place he is able to do it. The decision is, you can withdraw and wait to try another time **OR** you can choose to keep moving forward, you sit down at the table that the Lord has prepared for you, and the Enemy has to watch you feast.

You prepare a table before me in the presence of my enemies. You anoint my head with oil; my cup overflows. Psalm 23:5 (NIV)

The other less obvious time that we need to know how to deal with are opportunities.

The seed that fell among thorns stands for those who hear, but as they go on their way they are choked by life's worries, riches and pleasures, and they do not mature. Luke 8:14

It isn't just the hard parts of life that have the ability to derail us and keep us from maturing. It's the riches and pleasures as well as the worries.

He replied, "I saw Satan fall like lightning from heaven. I have given you authority to trample on snakes and scorpions and to overcome all the power of the enemy; nothing will harm you. However, do not rejoice that the spirits submit to you, but rejoice that your names are written in heaven." Luke 10:18-20 (NIV)

Here Jesus' disciples came back excited that they had been casting out demons. Jesus doesn't totally derail them because He doesn't want to kill their enthusiasm.

1. He empathizes with them. "I saw Satan fall..."
2. He reminds them that He is the one who gave them the ability and that it is theirs to wield.

3. He reroutes their enthusiasm to being about having their names written in the Lamb's book of life.

Jesus knows that having their attention on the high of the moment could derail them in times that they don't see things happen. This can be true with any success but seems easily perceived in the successes of business or ministry. Jesus reroutes their excitement to something that cannot be taken from them so that it is a solid foundation.

For no one can lay any foundation other than the one already laid, which is Jesus Christ. 1 Corinthians 3:11 (NIV)

Things to consider when facing the ups and downs.

For to us a child is born, to us a son is given, and the government will be on his shoulders. And he will be called Wonderful Counselor, Mighty God, Everlasting Father, Prince of Peace. Isaiah 9:6 (NIV)

Ultimately, the Kingdom doesn't rest on your shoulders.

Matthew 6:25-34 tells us not to be anxious about anything. God cares about you more than the birds or the flowers, yet they don't worry about what they will eat or wear.

A very practical thought is that the rest of creation lives where it can thrive, near their food, where there is good shelter, around others of their species, etc.

1. **You weren't made to be everywhere, you were made to be somewhere.**
2. **You weren't made to be connected to everyone, you were made to be connected to someone.**
3. **Surely your goodness and love will follow me all the days of my life, and I will dwell in the house of the LORD forever. Psalm 23:6 (NIV)**

A.   This doesn't just mean it follows you around. The meaning in the original language is that it chases you down in a way that it overtakes you.

> 1. Stay aware of all the opportunities the Lord has put around you for everything you need. **(2 Peter 1:3)**

No temptation has overtaken you except what is common to mankind. And God is faithful; he will not let you be tempted beyond what you can bear. But when you are tempted, he will also provide a way out so that you can endure it. 1 Corinthians 10:13 (NIV)

Temptation is not only about that which we typically see as sin. It is missing the mark. It also is when we are not believing we were made "for a time such as this." Esther could have backed down.

Sin is when we don't believe that God is Who He says He is, we are who He says we are, and that He cares for us the way He says He cares for us. It's why Jesus went hard against unbelief. Paul could have decided to stop preaching the Gospel when he heard Agabus' prophecy about him going to prison.

Be careful about isolating when you're going through major ups or downs.

John 11:38-44 is the story of Jesus raising Lazarus from the dead. Jesus tells Lazarus to come out of the tomb, but then tells the community to take the grave clothes off him. Grave clothes keep you bound, blind, and looking dead. It is still the job of the community to take the grave clothes off us. We cannot mature in isolation.

Proverbs 27:17 "As iron sharpens iron, so one person sharpens another."
There are times when things feel especially rough, and the main thing is to maintain your relationship with God.

Therefore, put on the full armor of God, so that when the day of evil comes, you may be able to stand your ground, and after you have done everything, to stand. Ephesians 6:13

I am coming soon. Hold on to what you have, so that no one will take your crown. Revelation 3:11 (NIV) Here Jesus is speaking to the Church of Philadelphia. They were experiencing persecution. But Jesus tells them that He is making ways for them and that He is coming soon. His encouragement is for them to just make sure they hold on to what they have. **There are times that, after you've done what you can do, you just make sure that your life with God is being protected.**

God is using all of it.

For our light and momentary troubles are achieving for us an eternal glory that far outweighs them all. 2 Corinthians 4:17 (NIV) The eternal weight of glory is our relationship with Jesus and our maturing to look like Him. He is using all these things to bring us into that.

**Let perseverance finish its work so that you may be mature and complete, not lacking anything.
James 1:4 (NIV)**

And we know that in all things God works for the good of those who love him, who have been called according to his purpose. Romans 8:28 (NIV) Not everything is God's will, but He does use everything for our growth and relationship with Him.

Ultimately, God is less concerned with handling everything for us than He is us growing into people who look like Him and can handle anything. It doesn't make every season feel better, but if we let Him, He will build us to where that same season feels easier the next time. Rather than lifting three hundred pounds for us, He would rather build us to where we are able to lift three hundred pounds.

Everywhere is Good for Worship and the Gospel

All of life is a good place for worship and the Gospel. I would go a step further and say it is really the only way life makes sense because it is what we were made for. Our life on earth is a dual citizenship. Whatever we can imagine about what life in heaven with Jesus would be like, it is infinitely more than that, and we are supposed to play that out here in the physical realm.

In the center, around the throne, were four living creatures, and they were covered with eyes, in front and in back. The first living creature was like a lion, the second was like an ox, the third had a face like a man, the fourth was like a flying eagle. Each of the four living creatures had six wings and was covered with eyes all around, even under its wings. Day and night they never stop saying: "'Holy, holy, holy is the Lord God Almighty,'who was, and is, and is to come." Revelation 4:6-8 (NIV)

These beings explore everything there is to explore (eyes), and yet when they look at Jesus, it causes them to cry, "Holy!" They are saying, "We see everything there is to see, but there is nothing that's like You!"

For since the creation of the world God's invisible qualities— his eternal power and divine nature—have been clearly seen, being understood from what has been made, so that people are without excuse. Romans 1:20 (NIV)

"Lord, our Lord, how majestic is your name in all the earth! You have set your glory in the heavens... When I consider your heavens, the work of your fingers, the moon and the stars, which you have set in place, what is mankind that you are mindful of them, human beings that you care for them?" Psalm 8:1,3-4

This won't be an exhaustive list because there is just too much of God that is revealed in everyday life. But it is meant more to help set us in infatuation mode, infatuation with seeing God and with seeing His Kingdom manifest on the earth.

If we want to make an exhaustive list, besides the fact that it's impossible, there's no way our minds could even hold all the different revelations we could put in a teaching. Ultimately it would probably weigh you down more than help you out. But if you get in the mode of seeing God everywhere and knowing He reveals to you what is right for you at the time, there is an ongoing fountain of worship. It also will come as a natural lifestyle that is beneficial instead of someone who seeks revelation that sounds deep but has no real application.

The early Church fathers had some different ways they would gauge believers' maturity. One of them was that a person was becoming a mature believer when they saw God everywhere.

Worship is supposed to happen everywhere. It isn't intended to simply be a musical event that only a few people really know how to do. Worship is meant to be an all the time thing. The Hebrews didn't draw a line between the sacred and the secular. Their home life and work life was supposed to be seen as holy just like being in the temple was holy.

Therefore, I urge you, brothers and sisters, in view of God's mercy, to offer your bodies as a living sacrifice, holy and pleasing to God—this is your true and proper worship. Romans 12:1 (NIV)

Hear, O Israel: The Lord our God, the Lord is one. Love the Lord your God with all your heart and with all your soul and with all your strength. These commandments that I give you today are to be on your hearts. Impress them on your children. Talk about them when you sit at home and when you walk along the road, when you lie down and when you get up. Tie them as symbols

on your hands and bind them on your foreheads. Write them on the doorframes of your houses and on your gates. Deuteronomy 6:4-9

Just like the four living creatures in the book of Revelation, we are supposed to be in this state of constantly seeing what there is in creation, looking at the Creator, getting revelation of who He is, then getting a bigger, better picture of what that thing in creation is supposed to be or the fullness of what God intends with it, and have our minds and hearts blown which causes physical manifestations of praise and worship, and results in us putting our hands to work in having that display on the earth for others to see.

"When one of the Pharisees invited Jesus to have dinner with him, he went to the Pharisee's house and reclined at the table. A woman in that town who lived a sinful life learned that Jesus was eating at the Pharisee's house, so she came there with an alabaster jar of perfume. As she stood behind him at his feet weeping, she began to wet his feet with her tears. Then she wiped them with her hair, kissed them and poured perfume on them.

"When the Pharisee who had invited him saw this, he said to himself, 'If this man were a prophet, he would know who is touching him and what kind of woman she is—that she is a sinner.'

"Jesus answered him, 'Simon, I have something to tell you.'

"'Tell me, teacher,' he said. 'Two people owed money to a certain moneylender. One owed him five hundred denarii, and the other fifty. Neither of them had the money to pay him back, so he forgave the debts of both. Now which of them will love him more?' Simon replied, 'I suppose the one who had the bigger debt forgiven.' 'You have judged correctly,' Jesus said. "Then he turned toward the woman and said to Simon, 'Do you see this woman? I came into your house. You did not give me any water for my feet, but she wet my feet with her tears and

wiped them with her hair. You did not give me a kiss, but this woman, from the time I entered, has not stopped kissing my feet. You did not put oil on my head, but she has poured perfume on my feet. Therefore, I tell you, her many sins have been forgiven—as her great love has shown. But whoever has been forgiven little loves little.' Then Jesus said to her, 'Your sins are forgiven.' The other guests began to say among themselves, 'Who is this who even forgives sins?' Jesus said to the woman, 'Your faith has saved you; go in peace.'" Luke 7:36-50 (NIV)

1. She had a revelation of God's forgiveness and love for her.
2. It caused her to pour out something that was costly.
3. It made her weep. Yes, it causes emotional reactions.
4. It also made her carry out washing Jesus feet with her hair and pouring perfume on Him when nobody else had offered to wash His feet.
5. This act has caused many to gain a deeper worship for Jesus, but also caused many who were there to be offended. Why? Because she took immediate, seemingly unprecedented action.
6. But Jesus also made a couple of huge statements about her actions.

    A. Wherever the Gospel was preached, her story would be told. Our love response to God becomes linked with His story. Why? Because that is the Gospel. Through Jesus, and God's forgiveness through Him, we have been brought back into a place where there is no separation. This is the Gospel. The full Gospel involves our response of worship.
    B. And secondly if you want to love much…realize how much you've been forgiven.

Preach the Gospel Everywhere! This doesn't just mean, in the traditional sense, go evangelize everywhere. It's the constant outpouring of the revelation of Jesus to others.

When Jesus came to the region of Caesarea Philippi, he asked his disciples, "Who do people say the Son of Man is?" They replied, "Some say John the Baptist; others say Elijah; and still others, Jeremiah or one of the prophets." "But what about you?" he asked. "Who do you say I am?" Simon Peter answered, "You are the Messiah, the Son of the living God." Jesus replied, "Blessed are you, Simon son of Jonah, for this was not revealed to you by flesh and blood, but by my Father in heaven. And I tell you that you are Peter, and on this rock I will build my church, and the gates of Hades will not overcome it. I will give you the keys of the kingdom of heaven; whatever you bind on earth will be bound in heaven, and whatever you loose on earth will be loosed in heaven." Then he ordered his disciples not to tell anyone that he was the Messiah. Matthew 16:13-20 (NIV)

When the Lord your God brings you into the land he swore to your fathers, to Abraham, Isaac and Jacob, to give you—a land with large, flourishing cities you did not build, houses filled with all kinds of good things you did not provide, wells you did not dig, and vineyards and olive groves you did not plant— then when you eat and are satisfied, be careful that you do not forget the Lord, who brought you out of Egypt, out of the land of slavery. Deuteronomy 6:10-12

Just like Mary, getting the revelation should cause us to pour out our love to the Lord, even in ways that are costly and that cause others to be offended.

You prepare a table before me in the presence of my enemies. You anoint my head with oil; my cup overflows. Psalm 23:5
When a cup overflows it goes down onto the table and starts covering everything else. Others could hold their cups underneath and get the same drink you're having. We should be in a constant state of getting our cups in places to be filled, many times under the cups of others, so that others can put their cups under ours.

Living in this way is the easy yoke and light burden that Jesus talked about. We talk about His goodness. People have needed to hear that. Therefore, they become filled. We see them start growing and are amazed by their growth. We tell them. They tell us that it was because of how we are. We are amazed, joyful, and thankful that the Lord used us without even our knowledge.

Living like this causes a response from people. When you speak about the goodness of God, it is the most natural, holistic way to minister. People will listen a lot more easily whether they agree or not. But people will love it or reject it. It is the way of an invading Kingdom for people to either accept it or try to fight it. Those who receive it do so because they want that infatuation relationship, they see you have with Jesus. "I've been to church...but I want what I see going on with you." It knocks out the preconceived ideas about religion, that it's stoic, uptight, and grumpy.

We have to get a much larger idea of what God has always intended for us and the Gospel and worship in our lives. Ministry doesn't just take place once or twice a week from a stage. Vocational ministers are not supposed to be your only source for spiritual food.

The work of the Five Fold Offices of the Church is to equip the Body to do the work of Christ. This means we are supposed to be getting trained to carry this out in our homes, at our jobs, when we are shopping, etc.

They devoted themselves to the apostles' teaching and to fellowship, to the breaking of bread and to prayer. Everyone was filled with awe at the many wonders and signs performed by the apostles. All the believers were together and had everything in common. They sold property and possessions to give to anyone who had need. Every day they continued to meet together in the temple courts. They broke bread in their homes and ate together with glad and sincere hearts, praising God and enjoying the favor of all the people. And the Lord

added to their number daily those who were being saved. Acts 2:42-47

Instead of just seeing ministry on a stage in a church, what are some other ways we could see people ministering and doing the Gospel?

1. Grandma taking care of her grandkids while her single child works extra jobs. She has the ability to be and preach Jesus to those kids in an impactful way more than almost anyone.
2. Teachers taking time with kids and displaying different aspects of the Kingdom that many of them never see.
3. A handyman that shows up to fix something at a house but not only does the job well but brings joy into a tough situation and lets them know that God is good.
4. But it is also ministering to the poor, casting out demons, healing the sick, etc.

Luke 10:1-11 is a great scripture on how to spread the Gospel relationally.

1. Let them know you've come in peace.
2. Fellowship with them.
3. Heal the sick among them. Take care of their needs.
4. Let them know the Kingdom has come near.
5. This a great time to give people words of knowledge as well.

The story of Stephen is also an amazing picture of everyday ministry that turned into evangelism. He was simply waiting tables but moved so much in the gifts of the Spirit that the Jews killed him, and he kept evangelizing and smiling while they did it.

The real takeaway I want us to grab from this lesson is to see God everywhere, but to declare that and act upon it in a way that it manifests around us all day every day.

Lastly, if you really want this to flow from you naturally, you need to see that your whole life is supernatural. Know that nothing in your life is normal. Everything you see was made from nothing, and that is not normal. God imagined a picture of you, a physical being that would display His glory. Because He knew He was going to manifest that into the physical, He knew that He first needed a place for you to be, He created the earth and gave us all to each other so we could grow. He placed you at a specific time in history, at a specific place on the earth, around specific people. But it all started from nothing. Be in awe of the little things if you want to see the bigger things happen.

CONCLUSION

I know there has been a lot of information thrown out in this book. I will simply state again and again, I don't believe we have a Good Father that said, "Good luck figuring it out." Even evil fathers don't do that. He made us in a specific way, and He made creation to work in specific ways. Faith and wisdom don't work apart from each other; they work together. However, "Fear of the Lord is the beginning of all knowledge, but fools despise wisdom and instruction."

We start with the faith that the Lord knew what He was doing, and that His way is the only one that works. If we don't want to do that, we prove ourselves to be fools who just want our own desires over what the Lord has to say. Don't make it complicated. Get to know the Lord. As you get to know Him, tie yourself to Him more and more. Have a heart of "yes" to Him.

I hope that in the reading of this book, it helped see that life isn't that complex or difficult, that Jesus didn't make things overly complicated. They are very simple; it is our desires apart from His will that make them complicated. I hope you saw examples here that made you realize that you have seen the truths of the Bible in many different places in life already, but that maybe you just never connected those dots or had the verbiage for it. For me, that was what really opened me up to constantly obsessing about Jesus, knowing that He was speaking to me and guiding me in every part of life.

Friend, God is deeply interested in your everyday life. He isn't looking to create a once-a-week escape from it. He loves the time with your family and friends. He loves spending time with you at work. He is interested in the things going on in your community. He isn't trying to get you to escape them but to boldly face them and stand strong in them. He doesn't deny hardship but gives relationship (righteousness), peace, and joy precedence over hardship. When we don't seek Him in everyday life, our faith simply becomes an intellectual philosophy or vain attempt at religion.

Don't make it complicated. Don't think you need to know everything right now. He will give you the answers you need at the moment. Just get to know Him and follow Him right now. Whether or not you've always been listening, He has always been faithful to guide. He cannot help but be faithful to guiding you to who you were always created to be. He's that good!

APPENDIX

Bonus material: extra conversations from discipleship class

Delivery of the Gospel

This is my delivery of the Gospel that the Holy Spirit gave me when I started at the Union Gospel Mission. I knew that I would be dealing with people of many different backgrounds, including ones that believed the Gospel to be the thing for white people and they should have nothing to do with it.

The delivery given here is partially taken from Peter giving the Jewish history on the day of Pentecost, except that most of us aren't Jewish and would have no connection to that. The other concept built into this is that Paul when he went to Athens and he used the common ground that people were searching for God, that's why they had statues to many different ones.

"In the beginning, we all walked and talked face to face with God. When sin entered it created a gap. Ever since, every people group wanted to believe that they knew who God was, how to navigate the ups and downs of life, and that at the end of it we would go somewhere away from all the trouble to live with Him forever.

"But all any of us were doing was making terrible guesses. At one time, God became a man named Jesus to take away all of our guessing. He was the very image of the invisible God. Now we could know exactly who God is, what He is like, how He thinks and responds to us and the rest of creation. He lived just like you and me, but He did it perfectly. He was accompanied by miracles, signs, and wonders. And then He died on the cross for us, as us, for our sin, as our sin. He put all of the old stuff six feet under and then rose from the grave so that in Him creation could be completely reborn.

"All He says we must do is to believe He has paid that price for us and receive Him as our Lord so we can experience new life. Do you want to do that right now?" To be honest, to this point I have never had anyone say no, but if they say yes, I tell them this:

"I am going to help kickstart a conversation with you and Jesus and let you take it from there for a minute. Just talk to Him about where you have hurt and places you already know need to change. 'Jesus, thank you for dying and raising for me. I'm sorry I've tried to live life my way. It doesn't work. I want new life, and I give you authority to tell me how to live it.'" Then I let them have some time.

When I can tell they are winding down. I tell them this: "You know that God doesn't expect you to wait until you die to experience heaven, hear His voice, and see His power. Before Jesus rose to heaven, He said that God would send His Holy Spirit to come live inside of us. Would you like that to happen as well?" Again, I have yet to hear a no from this. I first pray, "Jesus, baptize them in your Holy Spirit." Then I say, "I am going to ask God a question, and I want you to give it a minute and then tell me what you heard. God, what do You want to tell this person right now?"

I give it a minute and then ask them what they heard. If it lines up with something I don't believe to be the Lord, I speak over them how I believe the Lord would speak. For instance, if they say, "He told me I've been so dirty." I don't totally say that's wrong, but I tell them, "If that's what you're hearing, I would like to finish that thought for you, so you know the Father's voice better. You have been dirty, but because of My Son, Jesus, you are now as white as snow." Then I say, "What else do you want to say to them?" And I wait.

The gist is that I will wait as much as I need to and rephrase or correct the hearing to make sure that it lines up with the Father's voice. But eventually, they will say something that I can tell is the Father's voice and I simply say, "You have just heard the Father's voice. Anything that doesn't sound like that, don't listen to it."

The first time we did this was with a Native American lady who had known nothing about Jesus because she had been told to stay away. But she had wanted to know. When we got to asking God what He wanted to say, she started to tear up. We asked her what He said, and she said, "He said welcome home My daughter." We were so excited because we really hadn't talked about Him being the Father nor about being home. But that initial release for them to hear the Father lets them know that now they can hear just fine and don't need to solely rely on us. It's no longer our faith, but their own.

Highlights of this Delivery
We walked with God until sin created separation.
Then we were all guessing so Jesus came to take away our guessing.

He lived like us but did it perfectly, died and rose to give us new life.
Do you believe He is your savior and want Him to be Lord?
Would you like to be baptized in His Holy Spirit?

What is sin or how does it work?
Sin works like this. One day my oldest son hit his younger brother for the first time. It was the first time he was really in trouble. Just minutes before, we had been playing together and he was loving spending time with his dad. But now, I yelled his name across the room and a look of terror came over his face. He ran and hid behind the couch and began to cry. I called his name and gently said, "Come here, bud." But he tried to stay hidden.

Immediately, it hit me…Adam. The voice of Dad, who had been playing with you and making you food, has now become a source of fear. You ran and hid. I still showed up, I still pursued, but your sin made you run and hide. I called out, not because I didn't know where you were physically, but I wanted to know where you were mentally. I wanted you to say where you were mentally so that we could address it together.

See, in many ways, we still react just like Adam and Eve. It is the human condition very often.

But did God leave us or create separation because of our sin? No! We did that! If Satan was already here, then we were placed into a situation that already had potential for confusion. It's as though I took my kids to a carnival. It's really fun, but it has the potential for confusion.

Let's say my oldest son hits one of my other sons. Imagine I said, "That's it! I'm leaving you here alone in this confusion where anything else can happen to you." I would probably get my kids taken away from me. I would be a horrible parent for that, but many of us have been taught to give that attribute to God.

Now instead, let's say I swat my son, spank him, discipline him however seems fitting. I know that in his frustration and anger he would try to run and get away from the family. He would try to create distance. But I would need to hold his hand to make sure that he couldn't. Again, I know my son, and he would turn his back to my back so that in his mind he would create a gap between us, just like Paul says in Colossians 1:21 that we became enemies of God in our minds because of our evil behavior.

Now, we are at a carnival, and being a good dad, I'm not going to let one person ruin the day for everyone. Therefore, I start moving the family along to the next attraction, ride, etc. The whole time, I am needing to hold onto my son's hand to ensure that he doesn't run off. In his mind, we are still back five or ten minutes ago where the incident occurred. I'm not. I just want the family to have a good time together and for him to be his fun self again.

This is many times what sin does to us and how the Father feels toward us in our sin. Our sin is what destroyed us. Our sin is what made us create a gap in our minds. Our sin is what makes us think our Father doesn't love us and then we get even angrier. But He isn't stuck back at when you did this or that! His discipline comes upon us in order that we would grow because He loves us. But all He is wanting is for us to stay with the family and enjoy His goodness!

What happened on the cross?

Much of our traditions line up with Jesus taking our punishment as though God needed a whipping boy or He couldn't possibly forgive us. Well, if that were the case, it wouldn't be forgiveness but revenge. The wages of sin are death. If you work for sin, you get paid with death. Jesus wasn't paying the price to God but paying the price to sin. How does this make sense? Let's break it down.

Jesus had absolutely zero need to die on the cross for us. Yet apparently there was a deep need for Him to die exactly the way He did because He asked in the Garden of Gethsemane if there was another way and apparently there wasn't. Then why was it badly needed to happen this way? Because we were the ones who needed Him to die like that, and out of His great love for us, He considered it pure joy to please the Father and bring us back into full relationship with the Trinity.

Why did we need it to happen that way? Because otherwise, we never would have believed He forgave us! We were the adulterers, murderers, thieves, etc.! We were the ones who liked to flaunt ourselves as know-it-alls when we know nothing, meanwhile, He came in meekness and humility! We deserved to be mocked, spit on, beaten, have a crown of thorns, carry our cross, and be nailed up on it bare to die!

When we sinned, we ran, hid, and tried to cover ourselves up. But when Jesus took on all the sin of the whole world that ever existed or ever would exist, He made sure that He was hung up bare in front of everyone where He could not get away from people seeing it. He took on all our guilt and all our shame. And this is why it says He despised the shame of the cross because He was feeling how we had felt all this time. He hated that we felt like running, hiding, and covering up. He hated that we felt distant.

If Jesus hadn't taken our place like that, we never would have believed we were forgiven. It wasn't about getting the Father to forgive us but to get us to believe we were forgiven. Imagine I had killed a guy's son in a terrible manner. Then imagine this dad came to me and said he forgave me. I probably wouldn't believe it. Then imagine he told me he was giving me a car and some money. I would feel it was a set up and that it was a set up for a bigger plan against me. Then if he came to pick me up and took me out to eat, I would think that at some point he would be taking me out into a field to leave me for dead. But then if someone else wanted revenge on me and he got in the way and died for me, I would probably start to believe he really forgave me.

See, it's not just that Jesus took our punishment for us. It's that He let us give Him the punishment that was meant for us. We needed it in order that we might believe we had been forgiven.

I would add that there is a difference between the price paid to be set free and the communication of forgiveness. Jesus did both on the cross. Jesus didn't pay the price to an angry God. He paid the price for sin and death because death is the wages for sin. He paid our old master to set us free.

But if we are set free and yet don't know that we are forgiven and can go back home, where are we left? The truth is, knowing that we are free without knowing we can return home would cause many to simply return to their old master. Therefore, Jesus also expressed God's forgiveness to the world. As Paul says, "The Father was in the Son reconciling the world to Himself."

The cross both paid for our freedom and gave us the invitation back home.

Who is the Holy Spirit?

The Holy Spirit is the Spirit of the Father and the Son. Jesus told us that it was better for us that He returned to the Father so that the Father would send us the Holy Spirit. In describing Him, Jesus said He would be another who is "just like Him." This means the Holy Spirit is exactly like Jesus.

If I was a disciple of Jesus when He was on earth and wanted to talk to Him about anything or ask Him a question, I can talk to the Holy Spirit the exact same way. If I don't believe Jesus would ignore me or tell me I needed to go fast for a month before He would answer me, then I don't believe the Holy Spirit does that either.

Then what does the Holy Spirit do? What are His jobs? Along with being our comforter and counselor, here are some of the main jobs:
He reminds us of everything Jesus said.
He leads us into all truth and teaches us regarding all things, even the deep things of God.
He reveals to us everything that belongs to Jesus so that we can carry out the work of Jesus on the earth.
When we don't know what to say, He speaks through us.
When we don't know what to pray, He prays for us.

Therefore, with the Holy Spirit there isn't any situation where we can say we couldn't do anything. We carry the Spirit of the Father and the Son, and He knows what to do and has the power to do it. If you are putting too much weight on yourself, remember that you can put that weight on Him. He can handle it all.

About The Author

Justin and Elly Heckel offer over 15 years of ministry experience in worship and team building across churches, prayer houses, non-profits, and revival events throughout the Midwest.

Heckel Ministries' vision is to ignite hearts with the love of God and empower individuals to recognize and worship His presence in every moment of life. Whether in moments of grand celebration or the quiet rhythms of daily living, Justin and Elly believe in celebrating the goodness of God.

Their family is not just a part of their lives; it is the foundation of their ministry. With three energetic boys, Zalen, Liam, and Judah, and their playful puppy Daisy, worship is truly a family affair. The Heckels are committed to creating a worshipful environment for their children, nurturing their spiritual growth, and embodying family values within their church community.

Since moving to South Dakota, the Heckels started a church in their home called His Presence.

In addition to their mission work, Justin is a published author, known for his book *"Spiritual Warrior: Revelations of God Through Fighting."* He also uses his background in Martial Arts and Weightlifting to mentor and inspire local youth and young adults. Elly, a Digital Marketing and Brand Specialist, amplifies messages of love and faith through her expertise.

Support: The Heckels' mission is to strengthen individuals, families, and local churches in their journey of faith, ultimately advancing the Kingdom of God in their communities. To achieve this, they have specific financial needs, such as supporting travel for outreach and improving their online training and mentoring capabilities. By sowing into their ministry, you become a vital part of this transformative work. There are various ways to contribute, from purchasing Spiritual Warrior merchandise or their book *"Our Family Portrait,"* to supporting them through PayPal, CashApp, or Venmo at $HeckelMin. Your generosity, whether through giving, sharing, or prayer, is deeply appreciated and helps them continue their mission. Thank you, and may God bless you abundantly!

Learn more about their music on Youtube or Facebook at Heckel Ministries or His Presence Sioux Falls.

Acknowledgments

Thank you to everyone throughout the years who poured into us and encouraged us both as ministers and as a family.

www.ingramcontent.com/pod-product-compliance
Lightning Source LLC
Chambersburg PA
CBHW071214020426
42333CB00015B/1411